EM
EVOLUTION

An Invitation from the Council of We

Channeled by **Jennifer Elizabeth Moore**

author of *Empathic Mastery*

DEDICATION

May this book offer hope, support, and possibility.

For all empaths, creatives, dreamers, seekers, saviors, and sensitive souls,

For everyone who sees this world and knows it can be better,

For those who've hit rock bottom and lived to tell another tale,

For the champions of the lost and hopeless,

For the passionate instigators, fire starters, and courageous self-helpers,

These words are for you.

DISCLAIMER

Although the author and publisher have made every effort to ensure that the information in this book was correct at press time, the author and publisher do not assume and hereby disclaim any liability to any party for any loss, damage, or disruption caused by errors or omissions, whether such errors or omissions result from negligence, accident, or any other cause. Because of the dynamic nature of the Internet, any web addresses or links contained in this book may have changed since publication of this book and may no longer be valid.

The opinions and information shared in this book are based on the channeled guidance from the Council of We and the experience, teachings and creative inspiration of the author. Your mileage may vary. Please take what you like and leave the rest. This book is meant to serve as a tool for inspiration, encouragement and personal self discovery. It is not intended as a substitute for the medical advice of a licensed healthcare provider. The reader should consult a qualified medical professional in matters relating to her/his mental and physical health and particularly with respect to any symptoms that may require diagnosis or medical attention. The intent of the author is to share information to support you in your pursuit of empathic, emotional and spiritual wellness.

In the event that you use any of the information in this book for yourself or anyone else, the author and publisher assume no responsibility for your choices and actions.

COPYRIGHT

For permission requests, please inquire with the publisher at the address below.

Modern Medicine Lady LLC
P.O. Box 93 Pownal, ME 04069 USA

Book Design & Cover Image by Jennifer E Moore
Printed by Jennifer Elizabeth Moore
in Pownal, ME, USA

First Printing Edition 2024 Des'Tai Press

ISBN: 978-1-950984-10-7 (EBook)

ISBN: 978-1-950984-11-4 (Paperback)

ISBN: 978-1-950984-12-1 (Hardcover)

ISBN: 978-1-950984-13-8 (Audiobook)

ALSO BY JENNIFER ELIZABETH MOORE

BOOKS

Empathic Mastery: A 5-Step System to
Go from Emotional HOT MESS to Thriving Success

Empathic Mastery Diary: A Guided Journal to
Live As the Intuitive Badass You're Meant to Be

ORACLE DECKS

The Healing Tarot

The Sacred Empath Deck

The Empathic Mastery Oracle

A CHANNEL'S PRAYER

Divine Source

I offer myself willingly in service that I may be
a clear open channel for Thee.

Transmute and release any karma, ego,
assumptions, or distractions that would inhibit my
capacity to serve for the highest and greatest good.

Please guide me.

Please lead me.

Please show me the way.

Guide my hands, my heart, my mind, and my voice.

Speak through me.

Allow me to transmit Thy messages,
good and clean.

--amen

CONTENTS

INTRODUCTION

In 2019, I took the backroads to Downeast Maine. I drove past verdant fields and tree-lined woods illuminated by the golden light that precedes sunset on a perfect day in July. Sprawling farmhouses, charming cottages, and well-appointed colonials dotted the landscape. I was heading to a writing retreat on the Penobscot Bay. For six glorious, uninterrupted days, I would gather with an intimate group of colleagues and friends to focus on writing and unleash my creativity. My book, *Empathic Mastery*, was in its final editing stages. I was gearing up for its launch in early autumn.

The U.S. presidential election loomed a year ahead, but blue and red campaign signs already littered the roadside. Each one spiked a mixture of anxious hope and dread. I sensed that big things were on the horizon. It felt like something huge was coming. An urgency burned in my gut as I leaned into my mission to serve other highly sensitive empaths.

Empathic Mastery was born amidst a whirlwind of activity and excitement. I had all kinds of plans for where to focus next. Perhaps you've heard the saying, "Man plans, God laughs"? Within weeks of the book's release, my father's health declined rapidly. I dropped everything to join my family for a final sendoff filled with love, tender kisses, and a sweetness I'll always remember. Except, instead of dying, he rallied. The holiday season began, and I started wending my way back to my goals.

2020 was going to be my year. Finally, all the time, effort, and work I'd devoted to understanding and addressing the challenges empaths face was ready to be shared with the world. New levels of magic and possibility were within my grasp. Then, on December 27th, 2019, two days after my birthday, my pug, Bob, and I stepped outside for a walk. As soon as my snow boot touched the icy granite, I knew I was going down. My legs slid out from under me. As I fell backward, I could hear the resounding clang of my own head smashing against a propane tank that fuels our kitchen stove. Though the whole thing took less than a minute, the aftermath still reverberates. I'd sustained what some would call a "mild" concussion. I often joke that I wouldn't want to know what spicy is if this was mild. I spent the next two weeks lying quietly in dim rooms. I could not read without feeling weird. Computer screens and bright lights hurt my eyes and mind. I could only listen to audiobooks and watch reruns of the simple, amber-tinted sitcom *Psych*. My life had come to a standstill. Little did I know that the lockdown I'd been forced into foreshadowed the grinding halt our entire planet was about to experience.

By mid-March, the COVID pandemic had arrived with a vengeance. Conflicting information, divisive rhetoric, and toxic debates bloomed throughout the media, the internet, and local and international communities. Waves of fear, confusion, and unidentifiable intensity moved through me daily. I'd awaken in the wee hours before dawn feeling plugged into an electrical socket. The experience felt both holy and profane. On the one hand, everything was sharper, brighter, and more saturated than usual. On the other, I felt bereft of divine comfort as I stared at a ceiling of drywall and paint. I could not tell if I was having a panic attack, on the verge of dying, or experiencing what some refer to as "ascension symptoms." Though I was often able to drift back to sleep for a few more hours, I would awaken shaken and confused.

I'd lost my bearings. I stood amid a swirling, purple-gray fog that threatened to consume me. Though I was safely sheltering in place and able to continue working online with my students and clients, I, like many others, was brimming with a sense of foreboding. Then, in May of 2020, my father, John, contracted COVID in his memory care facility. At this point, there was little any of us could do. The world was in lockdown. A final visit to say goodbye was not in the cards for us. After only a few days, he died peacefully. He was among the first 10,000 souls to die from COVID-19 in the United States. His body was delivered to the crematorium, and his obituary was published in the local papers. We then waited for a time we could safely gather to scatter his ashes and honor his memory with lobster and tales of the open seas.

I won't lie. The loss of my father to the pandemic significantly informed my perception of the world. On one hand, I understood that it was his time. He'd had a good long run. Dementia had already robbed him of his conscious mind and able body. On the other, I grieved and worried. I experienced a cocktail of emotions every time I encountered the denial of the disease that took my dad. However, there was a third hand. Until I began to experience it, I had no idea that my father's death would initiate a total recalibration of my energy system. I'd suddenly become the terminal point on my paternal line. There was no longer a generation between me and death. The veil between the worlds of the living and the dead had permanently thinned for me. I'd reach out to my father, and he'd reach back.

Those years were some of the most remarkable and dreadful I've witnessed in this lifetime. I experienced moments of profound grace, as well as periods of getting sucked into the void. I leaned even more deeply into my relationship with the divine to navigate this uncertain world.

Shortly after I sustained my concussion, Luis, the deceased uncle of a dear friend for whom I'd served as a medium in the past, came through to insist I pray the rosary to help my brain heal. He'd been encouraging me to pray the rosary for a few years, but as a non-catholic with little knowledge of the actual practice, I kept putting him off. Between my own witch wound from past lives of persecution and my mother's vitriol towards all things religious (especially Catholic), praying the rosary was one of the last things I'd imagined this earth-centered, tree-hugging, energy-healing, universalist, shamanic practitioner, empath, and witch would ever do. But I was desperate, and Luis was adamant that praying the rosary would help reboot my scrambled brain in a way nothing else would. I became willing to try, so I created a modified rosary for myself. I configured it with seven Maters instead of the traditional ten used for each decade, and I used my own prayers in lieu of the Hail Marys and Our Fathers. I did this for a week or so, and then Luis told me to ask his niece for one of his rosaries. She gave me one that she'd purchased for him at the Vatican decades earlier. I begrudgingly began to pray with his traditional black rosary but still used my own prayers. This new prayer practice helped. However, it felt like something was missing. Little did I know where I was being led.

I'd always loved beads and beading, so as a lifelong artist and maker, I started to make more rosaries. I played with colors and created sets of prayer beads to represent different aspects of the Divine Feminine. I posted photos of my new creations on social media. A random stranger happened to see one of these pictures and suggested I check out a book called *The Way of the Rose*. This book spoke to my heart and simultaneously reflected my personal experience. It validated a path I'd straddled most of my life between earth-centered spirituality and my adoration of the Blessed Mother Mary. From my late teens, I'd been collecting

Madonna statues and images. However, I didn't recognize the correlation between my beloved Mary and praying the rosary. This book, which was "dedicated to the forgotten earth wisdom of the rosary... and to the Lady, by any name you like to call Her," pulled back the veil to reveal the ancient pagan roots of praying to our Great Mother using beads to guide the practice.

As both a third-degree Wiccan high priestess and the graduate of the oldest protestant seminary in the United States, I often found that I was too witchy for the Christians but too much of a Mystic Christian for the pagans. This book articulated what I knew in my bones. Previously, rosaries had been relegated to the penance of my mother's devout childhood. Now, it was a means for me to commune with the Goddess. The book mentioned a growing community of devotees who prayed together with this approach. I quickly found the online Way of the Rose community and their soul-nourishing prayer circles. Eager to connect with others, I attended my first online prayer circle in the spring of 2020 and became a host for a regular meeting soon afterward.

In addition to traditional prayers and personal petitions to our Blessed Mother, the meetings dedicate a final round of prayers to our ancestors. With this practice of calling upon our beloved (and sometimes not-so-beloved) dead, my connection increased, not only with my father but with many other unseen helpers as well. Interestingly, it was through this practice that I came to understand my connection with Luis on a deeper level. After a few months of praying with his beads, I came to realize how and why his spirit had come to me so easily years earlier. Prayer beads act like a phone that exists outside time and space. Luis met me decades before I met him, as he held that same set of wooden beads. My willingness to pray with his rosary completed that circuit.

During this time, I received guidance to host my podcast, write chapters for numerous books on healing, teach others energy healing techniques, and add to my rather full healer's toolbox by training in numerous additional modalities. I'd ground, connect with the divine, and focus on the task at hand. My work time was divided between clients, mentees, and students, writing, podcasting, and placing myself in the hot seat to receive mentoring and healing support myself. With all this time dedicated to healing and connecting with Spirit, I experienced many epiphanies and divine downloads. I cleared old patterns, inherited beliefs, and stuck, longstanding issues. It felt as though I'd finally turned the corner and vaporized the toxic atheism I'd been raised with.

But then the "yeah buts" and voices of doubt surfaced. Despite nearly forty years of experience as a psychic, energy healer, and spiritual teacher, I teetered between a sky of sacred magic and a chasm devoid of trust or awareness of anything beyond the physical form. Due to my upbringing, as well as my vulnerability to absorbing distress from this world, I experienced what a fellow member of our prayer community refers to as "an insecure attachment with the divine." However, despite seesawing between faith and fear, I continued to show up for my work and spiritual practice. I chose to "act as if," and when in doubt, I'd "feel the fear and do it anyway."

Perhaps my curiosity and inquisitive nature are both my blessing and my curse. Questions still arise for me about all the spiritual teachings that explain the meaning of life; the soul contracts we sign, and the reasons so many suffer on Earth. The skeptic in me has always struggled to make sense of spiritual platitudes that seem to bypass or dismiss the agonies so many endure. Though I studied metaphysics, healing modalities, and intuitive development for well over four decades, some concepts continued to irk me. This book, *Empathic Evolution,* is how I sought answers to questions that have plagued me and many of my friends, clients, mentees, and students.

Never had I attempted to channel anything of this magnitude before this. Though I had used my intuitive abilities to share information for over 40 years, it was usually relegated to sessions and classes where the oracle would speak through me as a co-conscious channel. Though I struggled with my faithless upbringing, I have always been able to dial the divine hotline and receive answers. These answers often come to my mind as fully formed words, concepts, and images. As an auditory processor, however, I must speak them out loud to bring them into the world. Instead of sitting with my laptop to write the first draft, the text started as channeled, spoken words.

Before I sat down and spoke it into form, the Council conveyed the structure to me. There were seven chapters. Each chapter would correspond to one of the seven primary chakras of our energy system. It would begin with the root as Safety and move up to the crown as Communion. Every topic was to be applied to the framework of the five steps of the Empathic Mastery System: Recognize, Release, Protect, Connect, and Act. I was instructed to use the Tarot deck I created to serve as a mirror for the information they had to share. Armed with these instructions, Nikki and I dove in.

Amazingly, we actually completed the entire first draft in a single week. With my audio files safely stored on a hard drive and in the cloud, I drove home elated and satisfied. I uploaded the transcripts from hours of channeled material into a document. I handed that over to my editor, Amy, to clean up. This was just the beginning. One of the things the Council made very clear was that they needed their messages to be accessible. The following is what they told me during a recording session:

> *"A note to those who channel: there are people who have the capacity to read bad writing, but most of you need information to be intelligible so that the message can penetrate. Please take the time to discern and edit. We encourage you to sort through what we say, clean up the grammar, and actually write or speak in complete sentences. We wish you to communicate with a structure that is accessible, palatable, and comprehensible."*

Amy, Nikki, The Council of We and I have devoted many hours combing through the original transcripts. We have edited and refined the content into a manuscript that keeps the integrity of the original message while also being as straightforward and approachable as possible. In addition to our stringent efforts to edit this book, I have also had to overcome my hesitation and resistance to publicly claiming my capacity for mediumship and my role as a channel for Divine Source.

Coming from a family that valued logic and science over faith and spiritual devotion, I've had to face my fair share of inner scrutiny and self-doubt. Because of my first-hand experience as an outsider in both secular and religious worlds, I've always felt the need to explain spiritual concepts in practical, logical, and accessible ways while simultaneously infusing reason and intellect with a sprinkle of fairy dust. I learned that how I experience the world is not necessarily how anyone else does. This has served as both my rose and my thorn. On the one hand, it has compelled me to approach my spiritual and healing work with rigorous impeccability. On the other, my baked-in skepticism, hesitation, and false belief that there is no point in sharing the information I receive has cost me years of valuable time.

At this point, with multiple books to my name, a podcast well into its fourth season, a Tarot, and two oracle decks (with additional ones in the works), I've obviously been able to override my resistance to some extent. However, my own self-doubt and karmic fears created a cloak of invisibility that has kept me safe from imagined naysayers and persecutors. *Empathic Evolution* is more significant than I am.

This book is where the rubber meets the road between my faith, devotion, and life-long intuitive gifts and the stale but persistent cynicism that has served as my emergency brake. To get this book to the form that you now read, it became imperative that I override the "itty bitty shitty committee" in my head, which sought to stop me from doing something so ridiculous.

"What will people think?"

"Who will find value in this?"

"What makes you think you are worthy?"

Despite all of this, I persisted. Slowly, incrementally, my fear has softened. Peace has filled my heart and radiated around me. The concerns I fretted over for most of my life have been lifted. Instead of reverting to the limits of my human mind that questions and resists nearly everything, my heart and soul have guided the process. As I went back through the manuscript with this newfound grace, I was struck by the synchronicities between the messages Amy and I were editing and the real time issues we simultaneously experienced.

Devastating events have occurred and continue to unfold. Some affect the whole planet. Some impact my entire country. Some brought great sadness and concern to my local community. As an empath, there have been many times when my sensitivity and vulnerability to taking on misery from the world have had me debilitated by fear, grief, and an inability to differentiate between my actual reality and the tragic struggles others are enduring. This time, things have been different. Though I've chosen to remain awake and aware of tragedies beyond anything I could control or solve, peace has dominated over succumbing to abject terror and despair. I believe my work today is to approach the world with love while bearing witness to the dreadful choices and actions our species continues to make and take.

Though this book is shorter than *Empathic Mastery*, the rough draft was extremely dense. Careful attention to every line was required to massage this volume into the form you are now reading. Often, the Council would speak in metaphor. Interestingly, they employed numerous biblical references, particularly about the Garden of Eden and humanity's fall from grace. This is their metaphor for millennia of perceiving ourselves as separate from the greater whole. Working on this has been both daunting and validating. At times, I have experienced so much doubt and fear of reproach that all I could do was acknowledge my stuff, seek support to address and heal it and wait to be ready for the next round of editing. Throughout this journey, I continued to give and receive lightwork sessions and to pray.

So, from this place, I share our book. I offer it with vulnerability, sincerity, and a genuine hope that the messages contained within it might help you as they have helped me. I invite you to approach this material with an open mind and heart. Please hold it with your own divine Council. Take what you like and leave the rest.

Before I sign off and pass the baton back to the Council of We, I will share one more thing: seek or pray for the willingness to be willing. When I started on my spiritual path in the mid-1980s, I was told to pray to be willing. Most often, this prayer would elicit defiance within me. A steel door would slam shut as I dug in my heels. To change habits and transform my life, I discovered the key was to ask instead for the willingness to be willing. These two requests may ask for the same thing, but I will tell you that the second can dissolve the most baked-on resistance, while the first will amplify it.

Here is the simple prayer that has carried me through everything:

> Mother/Father God, grant me the Grace
> to receive your Grace and
> show me the Beauty Way.
>
> And please grant me the willingness to be willing
> to walk that way as it is revealed.
> --amen

With this, I leave you to the Council of We.

WHO ARE WE?

Source Energy, Higher Power, Great Spirit, Divine Wisdom, The Holy Spirit, The Force, The Collective Unconscious, The Universal Mind, The All-Encompassing, The Great Mystery, The Universe, and All That Is are but a few of the words human beings have used to describe us over the millennia. We are the Infinite Presence that forms all that is beyond time and space. We contain everything: every memory, experience, thought, dream, emotion, sensation, and possibility of the entire cosmos. We Are That We Are, from the smallest particle of energy to the vastness of all existence.

As a living being, you are part of us. Our guidance and answers are held within your open heart and quiet mind. Your awareness of us relies on clarity and stillness. Though you are always of us and with us, it is your awareness and perception that ebbs and flows. You are born knowing us instinctively. However, as you become immersed in the chaos and complexity of human existence, many of you forget your connection with us. For many, the journey back to us starts when the pain of disconnection is greater than the fear of defying the pressure to comply with religious dogma or societal judgments. Communion with us requires three fundamental things: your capacity to surrender your ego centric mind, your willingness to open your heart and trust in us, and your discernment of the difference between your own mental and emotional triggers and agendas and our purest truth.

Jennifer, who is the channel of this book, was born aware of us. Our first confirmation of our plans for her was her birth date, three weeks early, on Christmas night. Though she was very curious, imaginative, and drawn to magic and wonder, her parents eschewed both religion and spirituality. Her formerly devout Catholic mother left the church to embrace atheism a few years before Jennifer was born. Her father, raised by agnostic intellectuals, was a secular humanist employed in the field of social work. Jennifer was often considered overly imaginative and dismissed instead of validated for her strong connection with us.

Her first wake-up call was when she survived a serious car accident at the age of 18. Although it took another five years for her to quit smoking, relinquish sugar, and start on a path of deeper recovery and healing, this near miss let her know there was an expiration date on her Get Out of Jail Free card. Many people are able to prolong embracing the path of recovery, but Jennifer was already too sad, lonely, and ensnared in an eating disorder to ignore it. Her low pain threshold and high rock bottom saved her life. Three weeks into her 23rd year, Jennifer chose us over resistance, ego, and fear. Through this thirty-eight-year journey, we have guided her, transmitted messages to her, and invited her to share our greater wisdom. It is her capacity to get out of the way that allowed us to dictate this entire book over the course of six days. We chose her to be a clear, open channel for us not only because of her enthusiasm, creativity, and intelligence but also because of her willingness to relinquish willfulness.

Claiming us despite her environment has been, and continues to be, one of her most significant life lessons. Jennifer's experience of the skeptical path of atheism is one of the reasons we chose her for this work. She was not raised within a system of blind faith. Instead, she learned to consider every insight or flash of inspiration with scrutiny before accepting it as truth. We give her information. Then, she takes the time to back it up with research. We appreciate Jennifer's willing yet mindful approach. She has witnessed the damage that rigid dogma can cause from either side of the religious spectrum. This has made impeccability and integrity her greatest priorities.

Because Jennifer was not raised within the constraints of a dogmatic religious system, she has had the freedom to take what feels aligned to her and leave the rest. At the age of nine, Jen experienced her first prophetic dream. The night her best friend's mother died a few states away, she had a nightmare in which her own mother had died. Even though Jennifer was only in the third grade, she grasped the correlation between her dream and her friend's reality. This served as her first invitation to learn more about extrasensory perception and awakened her desire for spiritual community. Jennifer spent her adolescence teaching Sunday School at her local Unitarian Universalist Fellowship, and by the age of nineteen, she had fully embraced her mystic path and obtained her first Tarot deck.

Jennifer initially called us "the Great Ones of the Tarot." During the early days, she'd use a guidebook, then ascertain and interpret the overarching patterns based on the meanings she found in those pages. She quickly found that information beyond those few paragraphs began to appear in her mind's eye shortly after calming her thoughts and grounding her energy. During our first decade together, we communicated primarily through the cards. This mainly was due to Jennifer's lack of confidence in her ability to tune in to us. However, over time, she learned how to connect with us with or without a deck of cards. The cards gradually fell to the wayside (except for special occasions when she still pulls them out).

What started as clairvoyant and claircognizant flashes with the cards eventually became access to our words. Over the years, we'd refer to ourselves simply as "We." A few years back, Jen asked us if we had a more formal name. We replied, "It does not matter, but if you need a name, you can call us the Council of We." This is the name she has used for us ever since.

What and who we really are is beyond mortal comprehension. We are the Alpha and the Omega. We are the I Am That I Am. We are the great mystery of All That Is. In the spring of 2022, we started offering Jennifer glimpses of this book. Much of it arose in the form of answers we provided to her questions about the nature of existence, specifically, why so many popular spiritual teachings felt hollow in the face of what appeared to be so much suffering.

By June, Jennifer accepted the call to write this book. We laid out exactly how it was to happen. She returned to the annual writing retreat she attends every July armed with a microphone, a deck of Healing Tarot cards, and a basic understanding of how she was to channel an entire book over a week. Jennifer's friend, spiritual sister, and book midwife, Nikki Starcat Shields, agreed to sit across from her as we spoke this entire book into being.

While we are the source of all the information contained in this book, Jennifer is the messenger. It is her voice we use to reach others attuned to this specific frequency. We also communicate with many other spiritual seekers, lightworkers, channels, and mediums to convey our message in a multitude of additional voices. If you are holding this book in your hands or listening to a recording of it, we suggest that you are one of those for whom this book was written. We understand that your species is going through a particularly challenging time. We offer this book to help you navigate.

A NOTE TO THE READER

As a channeled book, this is intended to be a sacred text. You do not need to fully understand them for the power of these words to affect you. This was written as an invocation, prayer, and spell designed to transmute imbalance and misalignment into grace. Every section contains seeds created to activate awareness, light, and revelation for you. This is meant to be experienced and digested at a manageable pace. Please take your time. Consume this in little bites.

As you read, you may find yourself asking what's next. Perhaps you'll wonder how to do the work the Council of We invites you to embrace. While you will find meditations, prayers, and other exercises clearly marked in the primary text, all these passages are primarily meant for contemplation and exploration. Therefore, summaries, suggestions, and resources have been saved for additional sections at the end of this book.

CHAPTER ONE
THE ROOT: SAFETY

Many of you feel insecure, frightened, and confused because connection is how all living beings maintain a sense of safety. We wish we could make this easier for you, comfort your abject fear, relieve your rage and indignation, and soothe your heartbreak. We wish that you could trust that all will be well. Unfortunately, your species' sense of connection to All That Is has become distorted and severed. You have reached a point where you have so many distractions and activities that your ability to feel connected is inhibited.

Ever since the onset of the most recent millennium, challenging events have amplified your sense of impending crisis. With the outbreak of your global pandemic in 2020, so much distress, doubt, and division have occurred that ordinary solutions and conventional ways of connecting with Divine Source have ceased to work as they once did.

IT BEGINS WITH CONNECTION

We are inviting you to up your game. When you consider yourself as separate and alone, it inhibits your ability to feel safe. To thrive as a species and progress to the next link on your evolutionary chain, all human beings will have to expand their collective toolbox. You need more than the resources and practices that you have turned to for thousands of years.

Your lack of safety has incrementally increased, like the "frog in a pot of boiling water." This is the result of the gradual loss of awareness of your interconnection with all things. It started with the onset of patriarchy, the advancement of agriculture, and the subsequent siloing of resources. It expanded as you embraced your need to name and identify everything as other than yourselves and to assume dominion over all. The development of countless languages also magnified your sense of separation.

We remind you of the importance of being in connection with the web of life on Earth. We stress the necessity of a community that moves beyond membership in your own species and includes the other life forms with which you share your planet. For you to feel safe, it is imperative that you cease to perceive yourselves as separate. This era of exclusively identifying as solitary individuals with isolated nervous systems is expiring. In actuality, you act as nerve cells for the Earth. Each of you serves as an interconnected part of the neural net of this world. Imagine yourself as an individual cell in the body of this planet.

Your lived experience provides feedback to the larger organism, which is your Earth.

Every one of you is a being of light who has roots going all the way down to the heart of the earth and a radiant crown of light that ascends from your head into the heavens. While most of you only experience the physical body you inhabit and the egoic mind contained within it, this is a sliver of what you truly are.

You are a being of light. This only begins to convey the grandeur and magnificence of your true nature.

When you recognize that you are an embodiment of light, you become aware of your divine nature. We invite you to open your heart and welcome this connection. This awareness of your light is something we encourage you to cultivate. As your awareness expands, this pillar of light within you will activate accordingly.

Every one of you represents the marriage of Heaven and Earth. You are the children of this divine union. You are being invited to recognize that the experience of safety starts with connection. This begins with connection to the earth and awareness of your link to all the beings around you, but most especially with connection to yourself.

> Know that you are a part of everything.
> The world is all around you,
> but you are the core of your own universe.
>
> You were designed to be the center
> of your own compass.
>
> Recalibrate to this truth.

MIXED SIGNALS
& UNPROCESSED EMOTIONS

Many of you are not even connected to your own bodies, much less your own truth or your own reality. Sadly, because of this, you have lost the understanding of your deeper nature. This is why there is so much illness, misery, and imbalance on your planet. As highly sensitive, empathic beings, you are often told, "You are overreacting and taking things too personally." You are advised to get over it, to let it go, and to suppress your emotions. Thus, you try to modulate the information that comes to you.

You constantly push away the messages we send you. In the short term, it may feel safer to avoid the information. However in the long term, shutting it out and denying your awareness of what is around you inhibits your ability to feel safe. Repressed awareness and reactive interpretations distort everything. An accurate perception of the world is essential. Safety requires knowing what you feel and how and where you truly fit.

You also feel unsafe when you are in family systems or environments with people who attempt to suppress, deny, or ignore their own emotions. It is especially difficult when you encounter people who are in turmoil but instead declare, "Everything's fine!" This is profoundly harmful. It is harmful to everyone, but for those of you who are hyper-attuned outliers, the next step in the evolutionary chain becomes unbearable. Empaths are beings who absorb the thoughts, feelings, and sensations of the world around them but process all of it as if it were their own. This makes distinguishing what's theirs and what isn't extremely difficult.

When receiving mixed or artificial signals, it is easy to feel disembodied and entirely in your head. Artificial fragrances, electromagnetic frequencies, additives, synthetic fabrics, modern structures made of concrete, plastics, toxins, defective wiring, wifi – all of these things interfere with your true emotions. They inhibit your ability to receive and recognize accurate signals.

When you are unable to recognize accurate signals, you enter a state of stress, confusion and overwhelm. While we understand that eliminating all of these features of modern life is a tall order, we encourage you to become more mindful of how you engage with them.

One of the reasons you have become so out-of-body, dissociative, and disconnected is because of the way your culture treats infants. For many of you, from a very early age (perhaps even as soon as you came out of the womb), you received the message that it is not okay to be emotional. It is not okay to express yourself to the full extent of your feelings. You are taught that you need to tone it down and make them manageable. Emotions need to be homogenized and palatable. This has gone on for countless generations because your ancestors were also conditioned not to feel or express their emotions. When they notice a crying baby, they try to silence the infant.

Think about what happens when a baby cries. In many family settings, the general response is, "Oh dear, something is wrong!" The caregiver checks the diaper, offers them nourishment, holds the baby, and tries to comfort them. If the baby does not respond to any of these interventions, it is easy for the caregiver to feel distressed, get triggered, and become dysregulated. This is exacerbated when you don't know how to process your own discomfort or are never given permission just to cry and work things out.

Years ago, Jennifer knew a woman with a young, colicky infant. One day, the baby was having a particularly difficult time. He had been fed and was especially gassy. His pained shrieks activated his mother's anxiety. She held him against her chest and rapidly pounded on his back as she desperately repeated, "It's okay, baby, it's okay, baby, it's okay." Her infant only screamed louder. As this mother's nervous system became increasingly dysregulated, this baby's synchronized nervous system spiraled out as well. This created a feedback loop that was reinforced by their mutual discomfort. Sadly, nearly three and a half decades later, he is incapable of self-soothing. He cannot self-regulate or moderate his energy body. He is constantly triggered and "out of sorts." He often seeks comfort through drugs and alcohol or instigates fights and engages in drama to sustain his familiar sense of imbalance.

To release the energetic congestion and emotional upheaval that inhibits your ability to be grounded, you must feel your feelings. We are not simply referring to feeling your emotions. We also mean that you need to feel the sensation of the breeze blowing on your skin and be aware of the fragrances and odors coming to you from all directions. You need to be conscious of the light, the colors, and the sounds around you and to notice your place in the world at any given moment. This is about your capacity to be aware, on a sensory level, of everything that you are taking in.

Knowledge of your interconnection is vital. Growth and evolution require identifying your position in the greater universe and feeling connected to the life within and without you. Whether you are alone or spending time with other beings (from the simplest single-cell organism to all life in the multiverse), awareness of your connection is essential. Safety requires feeling secure enough to express your truth, to recognize and acknowledge your emotions, and let them flow. For you to be grounded and fully embodied, you need outlets for your emotions. Spend time in spaces where you can experience and express yourself without interference. This might involve dancing or other kinds of physical movement. For example, walking and swimming are wonderful ways to process emotions. It could be journaling or writing. You might express yourself through music, pick up a craft project, or create visual art. You could reach out to a trusted friend. It might mean laughing, crying, or going out and smashing some plates.

As you allow yourself to become more aware, your capacity to shift and release thoughts, feelings, and energy expands. Instead of thinking of release as fixing a problem, think of it as neither resisting nor forcing but rather simply allowing the movement of energy within your system. Safety arises from your awareness of your place in all things and your ability to identify yourself as a cell in the body of something substantially greater than your mere human form.

To reconnect with the divine, the earth, and the cosmos, we need you to increase your awareness of your true nature and your identity as an immortal soul inhabiting a human body.

YOU ARE CELLS IN HER BODY

Humans have a tendency to speak of Mother Earth as if she is separate from them, but especially that they are separate from her. You are all individual cells in her body. Her consciousness is the entire consciousness of this planet. As you evolve toward a higher level of knowing, it is not merely you who evolves in this knowing. It is also she who evolves with her knowing. You are currently so disconnected that you cannot recognize how she is also affected by this disconnection. Instead you regard her as the victim of your human failings and, simultaneously, as the answer, solution, and salvation: "Oh, if only I could connect to the Mother!" To connect with her, you must connect with yourself first because you are but an aspect of her.

You are a manifestation of what she is processing. Not only is your species learning the lesson of reconnection, but Mother

Earth is learning it, too. She is calling you all home. She is calling you back to your felt sense of yourselves as cells in her body. This is the paradox. As you look at yourselves as human beings, there is so much concern and conversation about how "we're the cause of climate change, we're the ones breaking everything, we're so bad, we're so greedy, we're so toxic, we're so wrong. We're heading to hell in a handbasket!"

This is not a problem being perpetrated solely by *you* upon *her*. Your Mother Earth is intoxicated. She is affected by your human behaviors, your disconnection, and your illusion of separation. Her current state is her reaction to your disconnection. Her consciousness is evolving through the experience of a dominant species that does not recognize itself as part of her.

You *are* a part of her. As living beings, you incarnate to understand separation and to evolve and grow as eternal souls. When you experience separation, you also experience the illusions of scarcity and lack. As you encounter these illusions, you get to go through all kinds of lessons and ultimately learn and grow from them. However, what often happens is that you end up struggling and diseased.

What if it is not only human beings going through this period of challenge and transformation? What if this is also the greater, overarching lesson for the consciousness of your entire planet? What if playing with disconnection and interconnection, toying with the need for separation and space, and the need for fusion and communion are all part of the plan?

At the very beginning of all things, there was nothing but the One. All was unified form, with no individuation or separation. There was no knowing oneself because there was no contrast or division. There was no nuance or variation. To experience the ecstatic bliss of life and the lessons of love that all beings in the multiverse are here to learn, you had to divide and lose your sense of oneness with everything. So, you split from Source, which allowed you to behold the spectrum, differentiate light from darkness, and perceive all the other variations. As you began to experience the myriad nuances, you also began to expand into all the smells, sounds, sensations, and colors around you. While you started as one thing that needed to divide to experience differentiation, you are now experiencing so many things that you are imploding back into the One. As your world becomes more complicated and filled with greater levels of chaos, distraction, and information, this rapid expansion is beginning to fold in upon itself.

Your planet is returning to the awareness of the *"I Am"* consciousness. This is simultaneously overlaid with the awareness of separation. Connection requires that you acknowledge the history of what you have been dealing with for 10,000 years and make reparations to address the harm your species has brought upon itself and the entire planet. Heal and recalibrate to the truth of what is: you are the cells in her body. You are part of the symptom, as well as the cause, but you are only a *part* of either.

As you are of her, your Mother Earth is part of the cause as well. She yearned to experience herself as distinct from the whole. To understand existence and to be able to grasp the many thoughts and forms, Mother Earth had to divide her consciousness and experience herself as individual parts. Each blade of grass has their own unique experience. Each tree has its own sentience. Every winged, finned, and legged creature has their own individuality. In order for Mother Earth to learn, understand and make sense of everything, she has had to become everything, all one and alone, simultaneously. This is both miraculous and challenging.

At this point in the timeline of your evolution, it is understandable that Mother Earth now approaches a point of chaos. You are hitting critical mass, entering a time of crisis, and approaching the moment of apocalypse. You are at this point because you have learned as much as you can possibly learn in the form you have assumed. You and your entire planet are about to embark on a massive evolutionary shift into a whole new way of experiencing yourselves.

So, what if, despite all the doomsayers, all the ways that people are so caught up in the human perspective that "we are destroying the planet," in truth, you are merely a blip on the radar, a microsecond in the measureless timeline of this Earth? What if you are part of an experiment that is not necessarily failing but rather coming to a conclusion? Imagine planet Earth has a fever, and the fever is on the verge of breaking. Imagine you are part of an ecosystem that is reaching the point where it needs to go fallow and implode before it can expand into something new. You are reaching that point now, but your narrative as human beings is filtered through the belief that you are the sole cause of it all. Yes, your species is part of the cause, but it is so much more complex than this.

This is the inevitable conclusion of an evolutionary process the Earth has been going through for millions of years. The fever ignited with the onset of civilization. It started when you broke away from your indigenous, tribal, hunter-gatherer, cave-dwelling, or nomadic cultures and built monuments that anchored you to one location and aggrandized your human dominion over Earth. You began to accumulate more than you needed, but instead of feeling secure with your silos of grain and fortresses of gold, scarcity took root in you, and modern civilization was born.

To restore true paradise and to return to the right relation with your planet, you will have to acknowledge that you have been living in Paradise Lost. Your species fell from grace and from the garden. You were separated from divine alignment and your sacred birthright.

COMPLETING THE EXPERIMENT

In March 2020, the comet NEOWISE was sighted, returning to this part of your solar system after approximately 5,000 years. The last time NEOWISE orbited nearby was around the time the great pyramids were built in Egypt. While humans have been domesticating animals and cultivating plants for nearly 12,000 years, NEOWISE correlates with the expansion of patriarchy and its amplified form of dominion and control. The comet appeared again in 2020, a harbinger of the fever pitch you are now experiencing. It heralded the onset of a global pandemic and eruptions of political, social, and climate crises. You witnessed humans perishing from disease, gun violence, and divisive hatred. It is no coincidence that NEOWISE returned as an international lockdown was initiated. NEOWISE heralded both the inception and the completion of this experiment you have needed to go through as a species and as a planet.

What if, in the bigger picture, all will be well? Your bodies are temporary and designed to perish. When you begin to recognize yourselves as cells in the body of an Earth that is constantly renewing, regenerating, and recycling, you cease to clutch at the need to protect your individual existence. One cell dies, and a new cell grows. When you brush or comb your hair, dead hair falls out. Even though you may lose hair, you are not without hair. Hair constantly regrows and replaces itself. Like your hair, your bodies die and are replaced. For you to feel authentically safe and protected, you must embrace the inevitability of your death. As you integrate this, you are able to flow with the grace of knowing that this bodily experience is fleeting. You have nothing to lose. You will die. That is guaranteed. There is no appropriate way to stay in a human body for the rest of eternity. Your bodies are meant to expire. This is not a bug in the system. It is actually a design feature that allows your souls to evolve and grow.

Acknowledge the lessons that have arisen from all the trials, tribulations, and triumphs of the last 10,000 years. As you learn, we bid you to decolonize yourselves from all the human centered, patriarchal, and hierarchical systems in which you have been raised. We invite you to redefine your understanding of the world and shift away from prioritizing the bottom line, productivity, and the need to be constantly thinking in terms of the almighty dollar. Instead, we welcome you back to the truth of what you are: an interconnected spark in the web of life, a cell in the body of this Earth.

This is going to require work. Your world is addicted to accumulation for its own sake. Your culture has been inculcated with the need for the rat race. You have been programmed to believe you must put on blinders and entrain with a system that tells you, "You have gotta make the money." This affects even those of you who cultivate a state of receptivity and recognize that you are immortal souls here to work through your lessons.

You live in a body for a brief period of time, then die and transcend your physical form. There are those who choose deliberately to die when their time comes. They choose to accept their fate with grace completely. There is no kicking and screaming, no fighting, no telling themselves, "I'm a failure if I don't fight this disease!" There is no resignation either. Instead, there is a peaceful acceptance of the inevitable. These people can affirm, "I have lived the life I came here to live; my body has come to its end, and I shall now return to the great Cosmos." They will go back to the Akashic Record Halls, the Healing Temples, and dimensions beyond this mortal existence. They will get to review their lifetime, see what they did well and what they could have done better, and then make choices for their next incarnation.

The gift of this game called Life is that every 0–120 years, you get to renew and recycle. With every new incarnation, you get a redo. If your heart can access this, if you can feel this in your bones, then suddenly the urgency to survive and worries such as, "Oh my God, I'm not going to be able to pay my electric bill," subside into perspective. Certainly, you might be late paying for electricity. This might be hard for a few days or months. Your fear of financial insecurity might last even longer. No matter what misery you endure – even if it is completely paralyzing – these circumstances are temporary.

We are not saying that the misery of uncertainty and lack is not sheer agony for human beings. Your sense of individuality and dysregulation makes the experience of distress awful. However, empaths are the next link in the evolutionary chain. Empaths' capacity to feel the magnitude of thoughts, feelings, and energy that exceeds their own is expanding. You are all beginning to develop a greater capacity to sense the feelings of others instead of just engaging with your own limited egocentric (and often self-loathing) thoughts and anguish.

Because many of you are so distracted and caught up in illusion, most of what you experience is the darker side of human emotions. Your dominant emotions are anger, fear, and despair. You feel lost, overwhelmed, and isolated. Sadly, so many of your species do not experience much, if any, ease, elation, or pleasure. While many empaths feel cursed by their sensitivity because the strife of the world dominates their perception, some can experience substantially amplified pleasure. This is one of the reasons empaths tend to bond and fall in love quickly. We also suggest that many creatives are highly sensitive and empathic, with a capacity to generate joy. Often, musicians, dancers, actors, and other performers have the ability to project their art outward and then experience the bliss of the entire audience coming back to them. This capacity for exponential delight is the other side of being an empath. This is the blessing of your sensitivity.

The illusion of separation is dissolving, and your shells of individuality are being dismantled. A broader spectrum of emotion is becoming available to all as more human beings are born empaths or begin to awaken to their empathic sensitivities. You start to gain perspective, even toward your greatest torments. There are now more than eight billion human beings on the planet. Not only is there agony, but there is also ecstatic bliss happening in equal measure every single moment. While you are feeling the anguish of a person sobbing over the body of their dead child, you can also sense the wonder of a mother holding her brand new baby or the ecstasy of a lover gazing into the eyes of their beloved for the first time.

All of this is temporary. All of it is fleeting. All of it will dissolve and return to Source again and again and again. If you are listening to us or reading this book and thinking, "Yeah, that all sounds nice, but it also sounds like bullshit. You have no idea how awful my life is," we would like to suggest that you learn techniques to recall past lives.

We will let you in on a little secret: when you can recall dying in another lifetime, you are experiencing it as a memory – *as a soul who survived it.* Jennifer recalls being burned at the stake. She remembers being entombed with her sister priestesses in an ancient Egyptian temple. She has been eviscerated and thrown to the lions. She has experienced countless unpleasant deaths. Yet even though she remembers all of these (and they were ghastly), *she is still here.*

When you can recall not only your moment of death but also your crossing over afterward, it allows you to trust that even though it may have been dreadful, it is not all there is. You often carry traumatic past life memories as congestion in your physical and energetic bodies. You bring these forward into your current lifetime. If you have unresolved witch wound trauma, heretic trauma, slave trauma, war trauma – really, unresolved trauma of any kind – it will impact your ability to feel safe and trust life. When you can access the timelessness of your aliveness, you can return to breathing into the numinous and connecting with a force that is much greater than yourself.

SURRENDER TO YOUR DESTINY

When your ego is driving the bus, it defines what you want and need. You may be full of disappointment for a life you had hoped to live. You may find yourself invested in the transitory things you want that do not serve you. Nine times out of ten, you will not get them, or if you do, they will not fulfill your soul. Even if you create a vision board and spend every single day meditating, visualizing your magazine-perfect life in a beachfront mansion with the ideal spouse, three adorable children, and your dream car, these wishes are not necessarily in alignment with the universe. You human beings exist in a culture that has been separated from the greater perspective. You see things through the filter of your social conditioning. Instead of being given the entire manual, you have been handed a tattered, ripped-out section. The potential that you are able to imagine has been limited by the constraints of your culture.

Often, as you go out into the world and try to manifest, you make wishes from false expectations and misaligned desires that are based in avoidance, addiction, and reactive need. You are inevitably frustrated because you manifest things that do not work for you. Then, you gird your loins and wrap yourself up in a state of contraction that you experience as protection. You literally hold your breath. You move through life in a state of muscular and emotional strain. Your priority is merely to keep it together. With the amassing of material possessions and success, you dwell in a state of false safety. You are not actually protected. The need to preserve your wealth and status sends you into fight or flight, which contradicts true protection.

To feel safe in the world, even as it is right now, you need to break out of this contracted state. Stop trying to protect yourself by avoiding hurt and intense emotions. Allow things to flow and move instead of trying to control them. This is especially true of your efforts to control everything through your mind in an attempt to solve all your problems. Your mind is not in charge of protection. Your body is in charge of protection. Anytime you try to feel safe with your mind first, you will spiral out and amplify your insecurity. This is because your brain will search for patterns, try to find what it believes will save you, and form conclusions. It may appear to be contradictory, but protection and relaxation are interconnected. Most of you understand that to relax, it is essential that you feel safe. What you do not always realize is that to feel safe, you must relax.

One way to explain this is through the lens of martial arts. Skilled martial artists act from a grounded focus. They become surprisingly calm and relaxed in their practice. They are not frantic. They do not act from panic or agitation. They do not dwell in distress, nor do they succumb to a state of reactivity. Instead, the martial arts master exists in a state of heightened awareness from which they respond to take aligned action. They embody flow. They integrate logic, awareness, and leverage and are simultaneously guided by the instinctive reflexes they have honed through years of repetitive exercise. They do not overthink. They do not hold their breath. They do not seize up with tension or worry. They relax into the experience. They respond and adapt as each moment reveals itself.

As a species, this is how you are designed to live through everything. You were not designed to move through life overthinking. You were not meant to micromanage every last detail while tensing up, holding your breath, and anticipating every worst-case scenario. When you are in a state of protecting yourself from all the ghastliness you anticipate, your true capacity to be protected is inhibited. For you to actually be safe, you must fully surrender to your breath, energy, and the fact that you will die.

When you can stop focusing on the things you thought you wanted and stop looking at the way you believed life was supposed to be, you can begin to accept and receive what you were actually destined for.

Recognize how fleeting and temporary all things are. Often, you plant a seed in one life, but it does not flourish or flower until another one. Allow it to blossom in its own time, not yours. Please stop judging yourself for living life differently than the way you think you are supposed to. What if what you are doing right now is absolutely divine and perfect in the grand scheme of eternity? What if this is really a momentary blip that is so minute and so brief that it will ultimately be over before you know it?

YOUR PLACE IN THE FAMILY OF THINGS

Even though your human body may experience challenges, you are evolving to experience yourself as a cell in the body of Mother Earth. You are part of an exponentially expanding life form. It begins with atomic particles within everything. It expands into colonies of flora and fauna contained within your body and your own living form. It manifests as the interconnected tangle of life that makes up your planet. It continues as this Earth, which is a cell in the body of your solar system. The solar system is a cell in the body of this galaxy. The galaxy is a cell in the body of the universe. The universe is a cell in the body of the multiverse.

In relation to all of this, you are so tiny.

Whenever you strive to live in safety, mere strategy is not the solution. Constructing a rational plan is not the answer. When grounded safety is your priority, you must act from a greater vision. Act with the perspective of your position in the scheme of All That Is. Embrace your relationship to the whole picture. Understand your place in the family of things.

This is hard for human beings. It goes against thousands of years of programming that incites you to react instead of respond. You have been taught to grab instead of receive. You have been taught to hustle instead of flow. You have been taught to force instead of align. What we encourage you to do instead is to tune in to the frequency of trust, the frequency of "all will be well," and allow your life to unfold from this grace.

During the late 1300s, Julian of Norwich wrote the following chant: "All shall be well, and all shall be well, and all manner of things shall be well."

Right now, we wish to encourage you to place your hands over your heart.

As you are listening to or reading this book, simply notice your body. Notice how it feels to be in your body. Where might you be carrying tension?

Open your mouth, stretch your jaw muscles.

Let everything soften. Let your neck loosen. Now, notice your shoulders.

Breathe. Relax. Allow yourself to sink into gravity. Even if it feels as though your shoulders are already down, imagine them relaxing and dropping even more.

Continue to pay attention to the sensations in your body. Allow your elbows to drop. Let them release and rest as you lower them further. Relax and drop your hands. Give the weight of your body to the earth. Allow your belly to soften. Allow yourself to relax even more deeply into your body. Notice if you are carrying any remaining tension. Notice where you may feel tight or seized up.

Notice any thoughts that surface as you take this time to soften and relax. Simply acknowledge any ideas or feelings that may arise. You might tell yourself, "I hear you. I see you. I acknowledge you."

If there is any resistance or fear, try repeating the following question to yourself: "Would you be willing to relax and breathe anyway?" Allow the possibility that as you relax, you will be able to navigate any situation more effectively. Now pause and breathe. Sink further into gravity. Allow yourself to be supported by the surfaces of the earth that rise up to meet you.

Breathe. Inhale peace. Exhale static.

Inhale gentleness. Exhale strain.

Inhale love. Exhale love.

This is the frequency you need to inhabit. Your action is simply to focus on energy and frequency, not activity. We encourage you to dwell in trust, not anticipation. Allow yourself to simply be of this earth. Cultivate awareness of your connection to all your relations. Know exactly where you are on this planet. Know where you fit in your region: the town or city, the state and country you live in, the continent you live on. Know your place in the solar system, the galaxy, and the universe. When you know your place, you can relax into trust because you understand that you are but a speck of something so much greater and so much more eternal. You are part of something that is so utterly indestructible that even if you, as a human species, annihilate yourselves and bring harm to your planet, life will go on. As cells in the body of a being that is immortal and eternal, you, too, are an immortal and eternal part of the multiverse.

SELF-MEDICATING & OTHER COPING MECHANISMS

To feel safe, you need to look at the behaviors that sabotage your capacity to actually be safe. When you are in a state of discomfort, you self-soothe. If you do not have effective, healthy means for doing this, you will turn to alcohol, drugs, sex, shopping, sugar, food, engaging distractions, binge-watching programs, reading trashy novels, gambling, playing video games, or pouring all your time and energy into workaholism or codependent people pleasing. These behaviors are what some call addictions. We prefer to call them self-soothing mechanisms. You turn to all kinds of things in an attempt to mitigate and manage your distress. You may not know the exact reason you were triggered. Ironically, it is often by abstaining from the habit that you fully comprehend why you felt compelled to engage in it.

Each of these coping mechanisms brings temporary relief, but over time, they amplify the uncomfortable feelings you attempt to avoid. This is the paradox. You would not be doing them if they had not been the best solution you could find. The reason you turn to food, drugs, sex, alcohol, gambling – you name it – is because they are accessible resources or behaviors that bring relief. They do help. The problem is that the respite brought by learning to shut down your feelings, hold your breath, and contract away from your discomfort is only temporary. Relying on these mechanisms ultimately weakens your filters and shields and degrades your capacity to thrive and function in the world. It is a temporary solution to a chronic issue.

Actually, it is a temporary solution that causes a chronic issue. When you learn to function in a different way, the issue becomes temporary, and the solution becomes sustainable. We would like to offer a series of questions. We invite you to consider them and then simply acknowledge your answers with no judgment to yourself at all.

So we ask:

How are you self-soothing?

What is your go-to for relief?

What substances, habits, or behaviors do you turn to?

What is your relationship with food?

What is your relationship with alcohol?

What is your relationship with tobacco?

Cannabis?

Drugs?

Shopping?

Hoarding?

Romance?

Sex?

Pornography?

Gambling?

Thrill-seeking?

Gaming?

Social media?

Streaming Services or Television?

Arguing and fighting or getting caught in drama?

Sensory overload?

What is your relationship with sleep?

If you got up tomorrow and the worst possible thing that could ever happen to you occurred – your house burned to the ground, your most beloved person died, you suddenly lost your job, you went bankrupt, whatever it is for you – if you were to imagine that happening to you, what would you immediately turn to for relief? What is the thing about which you would say, "screw it, I'm going to do this anyway"?

What would you need for this *not* to be your go-to anymore? Let us work on finding better choices and solutions, ones that will allow you to feel safe in your body, safe in this universe, and safe in this split second of time where you exist as an immortal soul. Change starts by noticing that you are seeking to self-soothe. Recognize when you are in a state of distress. Start to become conscious of what activates your discomfort. Only after you become conscious of these behaviors can you choose a different and healthier alternative.

Choose to cultivate more mindfulness about your thoughts, feelings, energy, and actions. For example, you realize you just had a challenging conversation with your mom, boss, friend, etc. Now, you find yourself binge-watching an entire season of your favorite guilty pleasure. You recognize that you are activated, and now you are self-soothing. Add a brutal day at work, and you feel compelled to go to the bar for happy hour.

Right now, we are going to suggest something radical. A lot of people will tell you just to quit cold turkey. We say, instead of self-soothing unconsciously, start by choosing to do it deliberately. You have been using solutions that were the only ones that worked. Take back your power by owning your choice.

Sometimes, sudden withdrawal will cause rapid systemic dysregulation. Change often requires incremental decreases. Titrate. Cultivate mercy for yourself. Move to accepting and holding space for yourself. Coming into right relation with these behaviors is your goal. For some of you, this will be complete abstinence because one is too many, and a thousand is never enough. For others, it is the freedom to take it or leave it with no craving, charge, or white-knuckling.

BREAKING THE BINARY FEVER

Over the last century, the veil between the worlds of spirit and form has become thinner. You are able to see more colors and perceive more dimensions. As someone born at the tail end of the baby boom, Jennifer used to be one of the few people in her world who could pick up the thoughts, feelings, energy, and sensations surrounding her. She was one of the few members of her family who experienced prophetic dreams or sensed dead people. Now, this is becoming more and more common among you. The line between spirit and form, now and then, animate and inanimate, and sentient and insentient, is becoming finer.

Because you are human beings who have been programmed to view your existence through the lens of duality, this binary reality swings back and forth. It vacillates between expansion and contraction, abundance and scarcity, faith and fear. Sometimes, your species lives in a state of contraction, social and cultural restriction, and periods of constraint and control. These are followed by periods when doors open, perspective and knowledge broaden, your minds expand, and your rainbows increase. You are able to see, imagine, and conceive more.

From the pure, raw Stone Age, you have moved for tens of thousands of years through evolutions in consciousness, understanding, and awareness. All of you were born into the Information Age. It began as Analog and then became the Digital and Social Age in which you live today. Now, you are entering the Energetic or Light Age. You have expanded your spectrum of understanding and capacity to perceive. What if the increase in empathic sensitivity is part of your evolution? What if your capacity to perceive more allows you to recognize yourselves as something greater than your ego, body, or individuality? Perhaps then you will not have to cling so desperately to your limited perception of yourselves.

Your species is on the verge of breaking the binary fever. You are moving beyond the fluctuation between expansion and contraction, enlightenment and ignorance, and love and fear. This is why many people now have the ability to perceive energy and communicate with Spirit and the dead. Many of you are being born with memories from other lives intact. Many transgender and gender-fluid people are arriving on your planet at this time. Many souls are now incarnating from other worlds or dimensions where gender is irrelevant, while others have experienced so many incarnations as both female and male that they've transcended gender-conforming limitations.

Our prediction (and we started dictating this book to Jennifer in July of 2022) is that by the early- to mid-2030s, more and more people will be perceiving Spirit and having an awareness of the dead that walk among you. Where it used to be that only a fraction of your population could perceive dead people, this capacity will become increasingly common among you. You will grasp the illusion of death as you never have before. You will understand that slipping your mortal coil is but a transition from one state of being to another.

You will be in communion not only with living beings but with all that has ever existed. You will come to a connection with all things. Spirit is expanding and becoming more apparent; therefore, you will experience this to a much greater degree. Recently, Jennifer spoke with a living woman and her deceased husband about life after death. This woman and her husband communicate with ease. Not only could he talk to her, but he was also able to connect with Jen. He explained that just as living people can know that one person is in the kitchen while the other is in the living room, the living and the dead can occupy adjacent spaces but in different dimensions instead of other rooms. This couple's mission is to teach people that the old belief that death is a final destination is dissolving. Death, as most humans comprehend it, is an illusion. As the poet Henry Wadsworth Longfellow once wrote: "There is no Death! What seems so is transition." As you break free from your misunderstanding of death, you will begin to find a substantially better way of grasping the nature of your reality.

In her book, *Empathic Mastery*, Jennifer talked about how the humans living now are the 82nd monkeys. This was a reference to the "Hundredth Monkey Effect," originally introduced by Lyall Watson, which suggests that there is a tipping point when a population reaches critical mass. At that point, new perspectives and behaviors become the norm. Those of you who live today are not the hundredth monkeys. You are the precursors. You are the ones being led to the point where your world verges on cracking open into an entirely new way of being and experiencing reality. This is precarious. It is treacherous.

The old, entrenched, trauma-based reactivity that runs your planet right now is holding on for dear life. When you try to navigate life from fear and activation, your ability to navigate will be truncated and distorted. As long as you are seized up and triggered, you contract and react instead of relaxing and responding. Due to the nature of your nervous system, you cannot do anything else until your fight, flight or freeze response has been deactivated and your body feels safe.

Because trauma inhibits access to one's full capacity for reason, reactivity and illusion are what you know. This is what informs most peoples' current sense of reality. This trauma-based perspective aligns with scarcity. It knows the void of struggle, lack, and fear as truth. It believes that death is the final thing. Subsequently, you are compelled to protect yourselves from death at all costs. When you believe that protecting the body from death is the top priority, you will often react impulsively instead of responding with trust. When you can accept the fundamental truth that this body is going to die and become completely willing to die at your appointed time, miracles start to happen. Then you are living to live instead of living not to die. Then, you can find your way through.

Consider the contrast between Eastern martial arts and Western civilization's military approach. The former is often influenced by grounded acuity, while the latter is often driven by adrenaline and fear. Generally, this causes more collateral damage than the precise and leveraged hits taught in martial arts. The martial arts approach is about alignment, adaptation, and course correction, whereas Western warfare is often explosive and excessively destructive. The difference lies between reaction and response, emotional impulse and calm alertness, overwhelm and clarity. All of this is a manifestation of unresolved trauma. It is absolutely imperative for you, as a species, to do your work to heal that trauma. Heal the wounds that you have experienced during this lifetime and address the damage carried over from previous incarnations, as well as the long-standing suffering you have inherited from your ancestral lines.

This book is an invitation to use new tools, to try something different, to respond and relax instead of contracting and reacting. Do the work that you were born to do. If you are alive on the planet right now and reading or hearing this book, you are doing so because you have been called to be part of the solution. Your species is hitting critical mass. It is "go time." With over eight billion human inhabitants on your planet, your population has grown so large that there are more people than there have ever been at any other single period in history. As of 2022, a total of nearly 120 billion human beings have been born on this earth[1] throughout the history of humanity.

Humanity's current population comprises nearly 7% of your entire population since homo sapiens began to walk this earth almost 200 thousand years ago. It took from the year 1CE to 1750 CE for your population to more than double from 300 million to 750 million. In little more than a century, the nearly 1.6 billion humans inhabiting your planet in 1900 have more than quadrupled to over 8 billion today! The magnitude of this rapid increase is nearly inconceivable. You might imagine, as you consider these numbers, that many alive today have lived here numerous times before. Though you may not recall your

---

[1]   https://www.prb.org/articles/how-many-people-have-ever-lived-on-earth/

other lives, contained within you are all the memories, lessons, vows, agreements, and contracts from every incarnation you have inhabited.

We entreat you to join all the other awake, aware, and sensitive souls who were also born to do the work. What you will pass along to your great, great grandchildren is something that you can hardly conceive of right now. The New Earth being born is the promise of your prayers today. Please accept our invitation and commit to the healing, visioning, and creativity that will transform your world.

Instead of imagining this as an agonizing slog through your pain, let us offer you the possibility that this can be gentle, sweet, and even fun. Once you cut loose the dead weight of all the trauma you have all been carrying for thousands of years, what becomes possible is miraculous.

CHAPTER 2

THE VESSEL: PLEASURE

Throughout your everyday modern lives, you are contracted in empathic overwhelm and concern. You have so much information coming at you and so many people pleading for help that you often feel compelled to offer solutions that are completely outside your wheelhouse. While you have the agency to make a difference in this world, the level of responsibility that you take on is utterly disproportionate to what you are able to do as individuals. This level of concern, guilt, and responsibility impacts many of you and interferes with your ability to maintain a state of ease.

AN EQUAL MEASURE OF JOY

The first thing you need to work on is recognizing what is realistic for you, what is really yours, and what is not. To achieve ease, you must release burdens that do not belong to you. Let go of excessive concern for everything and everyone. When you are in this state of worry, you cease to be fully embodied. You cease to be in a state of ease. Instead, you block the channel, the ebb and flow, and the divine grace. You are meant for pleasure. You are meant for joy and creativity. You are meant for delight and bliss. You were designed to savor the experience of being embodied and alive, delighting in the beauties and wonders of this universe.

As you come into interconnection and awareness of how you are related to one another, you are getting bogged down. You experience a great deal of empathy for misery but not for joy. Many of you do not have empathy for pleasure. A very big part of your embodiment of the sensuous is learning how to cultivate empathy for the good side of things. There is a saying that "the squeaky wheel gets the grease." You have become really tuned in to the squeaky wheel of distress. This awareness generates even more distress. Only a small number of you are fully embodied and living in a state of ecstatic grace and bliss. To turn things around, you must claim your birthright to pleasure, your birthright to nourishment, community, creativity, and delight.

You exist in a state of anxiety for things that you cannot fully comprehend. Your capacity for prediction is also your Achilles' heel. You tend to use your ability to look forward in the timelines to anticipate what is to come, but you do it clouded with your own fears, shadowed by your assumptions and triggers from the past. Therefore, when you look forward to seeing a glimmer of the future, you perceive partial truths. This makes you suffer. You stop at the first scene of a multi-act play. You see a fraction of the story. You gather information through your limited perspective to form conclusions and predict outcomes to a future that you cannot accurately grasp.

The lens of societal conditioning, media-driven concern, and mortal insecurity constrains your sense of existence. Yet, in reality, you are so vast and so magnificent that you cannot conceive what you truly are. You possess the understanding of toddlers playing in the confines of your small backyard. You experience a fraction of the subtleties and nuances of all the things occurring at any given moment. You believe that you know what will happen and how this is all going to play out. You are making yourselves miserable! You peer through a dark, half-empty glass so you cannot even see what you have.

Some of this is the inherited legacy of more than 10,000 years of active patriarchy, long years of suppression of your sensuality, denial of your pleasure, and avoidance of your delight. This is the result of separation and disconnection. Many of you sleepwalk through your days in a state of self-flagellation and assumption. All the agonies you imagine, the fears you project, and the imminent crises you concern yourself with are not what you think they are. You persist in trying to know it all. You persist in trying to define it, attempting to make meaning of things that are too vast, too great, and too complex for you to understand.

Therefore, we suggest you recognize that you have only part of the equation right now. Consider the possibility that, for all the concern, sympathy, and absorbed sorrow for which you cultivate your compassion, there is also an equal measure of ecstatic bliss, delight, and joy. We invite you to align with the things that bring you pleasure. Start allowing yourself to relax into the moment. Allow yourself to be embodied. As you recognize the truth that there is an equal measure of joy and you start calibrating to this joy, you will begin to trust that you can collectively shift the tide and turn the struggle around.

While receiving our transmissions for this book, Jennifer became curious about the percentage of humans who identify as happy. She imagined that people who experience unbridled joy, ease, and pleasure, allowing themselves to go after their truest passion and deepest desires, make up a fairly small percentage of the population. Her imagined calculation was less than 5% of the entire human population. When Jennifer did some research, she was pleasantly surprised to learn that 64% of the global population surveyed identified as happy, which included 14% who claimed to be "very happy." These 14% are the ones who are living as we desire. While 14% is certainly better than 5%, this still leaves much room for improvement.

It is evident from the above that there are exceptions living to their full potential. There are people who are capable of states of bliss. However, many of you are not. You humans are mostly asleep and frozen in a nightmare. However, you are beginning to awaken to your divine birthright, galactic heritage, sovereignty, joy, and pleasure. You are being offered ecstasy that is absolutely yours to experience as a sentient being.

In the first chapter, we talked about the tendency to self-soothe. What you experience when you pick up a substance to find relief is a pale facsimile of actual delight. True pleasure is the antidote to self-soothing. It is the antidote to addiction and your struggles with pain. Embracing real bliss activates feelings of satisfaction and fulfillment. To embody this, it is vital that you identify what truly makes you happy. To access this birthright of pleasure and satisfaction you must acknowledge how you block it. So we have some questions for you:

What stops you from embracing your birthright to experience delight, pleasure, and joy?

How do you inhibit yourself from experiencing these things?

How do you withhold pleasure from yourself?

In what ways are you stopping yourself from saying yes?

Why?

Is it guilt?

Responsibility?

Legacies of family agreements or karmic wounds?

To embody the richness of life, you will need to shift from hustle to flow, from promotion to attraction, from pushing, forcing, trying, and clutching to allowing yourself to simply be. This release is not fiery or logical; it is the relinquishing of your effort to control everything in existence. It relies on your surrender of self-will. It requires willingness and the acceptance of grace. The energy we wish you to welcome is the energy of ease, embodiment, and trust. Trust requires feeling safe and grounded. Then, when you access trust, you can claim your sovereignty. To allow wealth and satisfaction into your life, it is imperative that you come to trust that there is a force greater than you, something larger than your own human foibles and your left-brained idea of how the universe unfolds. Trust is a vital piece of the equation for experiencing abundance, ease and wellbeing.

There are people in the world who make inconceivable amounts of money. Some even make over a billion dollars every week. They have access to all the things humans believe they need and want. But even with billions, they experience lack. In their endless pursuit to acquire more, they demonstrate to themselves and the world around them that what they have is not enough. Even with levels of wealth magnitudes beyond your human brain's understanding, these billionaires still pursue more.

Thriving is as much about *enoughness* as it is about trust. Your well-being relies on releasing the illusion that you need to cultivate more. When you have no sense of safety or trust, you feel compelled to pursue more. You are never enough. Nothing is adequate. No thing can meet your needs, so you are compelled to continuously seek more, enslaved by the rat race you have created for yourselves.

GLIMMERS OF DELIGHT

As we mentioned before, you have collectively reached a fever pitch that escalates daily. This is evident in your ceaseless levels of consumption. You witness the symptoms as islands of plastic in your oceans and artificial mountains of textiles, electronics, and discarded amusements rising across the land. If you are an entrepreneur who runs your own business, no matter where you are on your journey you face pressure to uplevel every year. Today, success has become conflated with growth. Every year, you must grow more. If you did not exceed the previous year, your stasis is regarded as a failure. This contradicts what you are really meant to do as human beings. This pressure puts you in a state of not-enoughness. It holds you back from your true, deep, abiding birthright, which is that there is plenty for all of you. There is abundance everywhere. You are enough. We are enough. They are enough.

The relentless quest for material goods and immeasurable financial wealth is, in truth, simply fear. We urge you to release this fear. We ask you to release your white-knuckled grip on security as your means to safety. We wish you to soften the clenching in your body and allow yourself to feel how you are held and supported by the earth beneath and beside you. We ask you to release the part of you that does not believe and is so focused on the future that you cannot access the present moment.

Another way to think about this chapter entitled "Pleasure" lies in the word "presence." Trust, ease, presence, and embodiment are essential to flourish. There is an old saying that "when you have one foot in the past and one foot in the future, you are pissing on the present." You have been sucked into a pattern of succumbing to past trauma that activates your current challenges and stress. Simultaneously, you project anticipation of more trauma into the future. As you straddle the traumas of the past and the imagined traumas of the future, you cannot recognize that, at this very moment, you are okay. If you are listening to or reading this book, it means that you are alive. It means that you are breathing. It means that chances are you have probably had at least one meal today. We imagine you are wearing clothing. We imagine that you are in some form of shelter. This means that you have survived everything that has led to this moment, and you are still here. Right now, at this very moment, you are okay.

When you come back into the moment, when you return to the here and now, you are able to sink into the little bits of delight and pleasure that nourish your soul. Many of you have been fed a media-driven idea of what pleasure looks like. You are exposed to artificial concepts of success, love, joy, and prosperity through your music, movies, TV shows, novels, social media, and more. As a result, you are vulnerable to distorted perceptions of what pleasure actually is. This is especially true for female pleasure. Consider some of your cultural portrayals: the forbidden decadent dessert, a luxurious bubble bath, romantic encounters that yield mind-boggling orgasms and lead to happily-ever-after fairy tale outcomes. You don't recognize how to embody pleasure in your own lives because you are looking for the diamond ring, the white picket fence, or the Big O. You have been taught to look for fireworks, for the extreme, dramatic crescendo, and the idea that true happiness should last forever. As a result, you deprive yourself of all the tiny delights that are available to you every single day.

As you relinquish fear and realign with trust in the moment, we invite you to turn away from the trauma of the past and your fearful projection into the future. This way, you will begin to find glimmers of joy and delight. It may be the experience of a child running to hug your calf because they are too little to reach your waist. It may be sharing a chocolate truffle with a friend and marveling at how delicious it is. Maybe it will be singing with a group and laughing as you mess up the lyrics. Maybe it will be standing outside for 30 seconds between one phone call and the next to feel the breeze on your skin and the sun warming your shoulders. Perhaps it will be reaching for your favorite blanket and sinking into the coziness that envelops you.

This is how to shift from concern to pleasure. This is how you will shift from being caught between the past and the future to being in the present. This is how you release your attachment to the past and your gripping terror about what is to come. This is how you find your way – by appreciating the small pleasures and letting go of that which no longer serves you.

Though you live in a time that may feel very precarious, you are still entitled to delight. You are still entitled to joy and pleasure. Claim space for yourself. Say "yes" to what matters to you and allow the world to find its way to you. Become proactive in defining and creating the container of your life. Define your space. Be deliberate when setting the table and welcoming the guests. Choose to allow love in. Choose to trust. Choose to believe in abundance. Choose to know that you are enough and that the world is enough.

For you to protect yourself and to trust, understanding how to do this is required. It is not simply learned by osmosis, mimicking the limited coping skills of your parents or guardians. Often, you were taught ineffective, inefficient ways to protect your-selves. You were led to believe that you should simply know how to do things. You should know how to raise children. You should know how to cook. You should know how to manage finances. You should know how to communicate. You should know how to study. You should know how to forgive. You should know how to pursue your heart's desire. Somehow, you should just know all of this, but until you have been given the proper tools and instruction, you simply don't. Grant yourself grace for all the things you were never taught. Know that it is okay not to know everything. Allow yourself to seek the information and resources that you need.

KNOWING YOUR "NO"

To come to an ever deeper trust and embodiment, you must learn to set boundaries. Learn to recognize what actually feels good and what is simply an itch, urge, or need to acquiesce. What do you truly desire? When do you need it? To flourish, you must know your limitations and boundaries. It is imperative that you know your "no" as clearly as you know your "yes." To say "yes," learn to say "no" first.

To safely live in a state of embodiment, you must not only trust the universe and trust that all will be well, but you must trust yourself, too. No amount of trusting something external to you is going to make any difference if you do not trust yourself. You will sabotage your joy, ease, and destiny because you do not trust yourself to set boundaries. If you cannot recognize when some-thing feels off or misaligned, if you do not want to do something and you agree to do it anyway, then you lose trust in yourself.

You must recognize what feels good to you. What do you actually desire? Women, in particular, have been socialized to become the object of desire and the source of pleasure but not to recognize their own desire or pleasure. To trust, to be fully embodied, to feel pleasure, and to be in a state of ease, grace, and flow, you must trust your ability to say "no."

Saying "no" is scary at first. Saying "no" is hard if you have never learned how to do it. Saying "no" is not an apology. Before you can say "no," you must recognize what feels right to you. Often, you feel this truth in your belly. Either there is a feeling of, "Yes, this is delicious, safe, good, and right," or "No, not so much."

> *How many times in your life have you said "yes" to things that you really didn't want?*

> *How many times did fear of disappointing someone else make you do, agree to, or go somewhere you really didn't want to?*

> *How many times has wanting to be good made you say "yes" when your body was screaming that this was not right at all?*

You must learn to honor yourself. You need to learn what your "no" is and how to express it with civility and strength. Identifying the "no" or "yes" in your body requires experimentation. Part of this is your ability to trust that if you don't like it, you can change your mind. This is very much about letting go of the idea that "you made your bed, now you must lie in it." You are not destined to spend the rest of your life in that bed. You are always allowed to experiment and course-correct. One of the things that inhibit your embodiment and claim to your rightful place in this world is the fear of failure. Shift your narrative from defining things as experiences of failure to experiments providing feedback, data, and opportunities. As you discover what you love and what you do not love, you can adapt accordingly.

As an immortal soul, it can sometimes seem as if you live a pointless life and then you die. In her last life, Jennifer was a relatively unknown chorus girl turned Hollywood "starlet" and mistress of a movie executive. She was mostly an extra, first in silent films and then in the talkies. She climbed her way up the ranks in the 1930s and '40s. By the time the '50s rolled around, she had lost her luster but maintained her status as a well-kept mistress. He bought her a car and a choice bungalow on the beach. Jennifer can still see the little house clearly, up on stilts looking out over the ocean. It was a beautiful, light-filled space with gauzy white curtains billowing in the breeze and cream-colored furniture with crystal and chrome accents. The briny scent of ocean air mixed with Chanel No. 5, tobacco smoke, and bourbon. Despite all this beauty, this former version of Jen's soul spent most of her time in a maudlin state of despair, drinking, smoking, and playing Russian roulette with her mother-of-pearl-handled Walther PPK. Her son, the illegitimate child of this married man, was taken very good care of by his "uncle." He went to the best Swiss boarding schools. He attended Oxford University in England. All of his life was set before him. Unfortunately, he didn't have a lot of regard for his mother. He actually had a fair bit of disdain for the lush she'd become and her wanton ways. He had nothing to gain from her, so he was gone. She was relegated to being a kept woman who had been left to collect dust. One of Jennifer's friends recently described a married man to whom she had been a long term, long distance romantic partner as "an absentee landlord." Jennifer's past life was very similar. If she saw the executive who provided for her once every two or three months, she was lucky. She was despondent and depressed. She also starved herself to try to stay thin and beautiful, eating half a TV dinner or half a can of tomato soup with a sliver of toast as her daily food ration. She drank most of her calories in the form of whiskey and smoked like it was going out of style. She'd smoke her Winstons and sit at her vanity or recline on her couch and stare out at the ocean. Though she was less than 50 yards from an exquisite beach, she rarely, if ever, went outside. By the late '50s, she was so beside herself with boredom, misery, and contempt for her self-proclaimed sins that she had nothing to keep her earthside. She was absolutely done. On the fall equinox of 1957, she put a gun to her head and, with little fanfare, she shot herself. She died, crossed over, and was born five years later in another body – the body that Jennifer inhabits now.

That life was rife with failure. Jennifer's past self did not realize her full potential or achieve more than a few fleeting moments of joy. She allowed her fear, insecurity, and history of trauma to block her ability to go forth and be radiant. Had she embraced her destiny, she would have experienced the glorious life she'd been born for. She would have become a true star of the silver screen. She would have eventually started her own production company. She would have created masterpieces, written screenplays, and directed and produced meaningful films by women, for women, that would have stood the test of time. Instead, she just stopped. In many ways, this was no harm/no foul because, as an immortal soul, that life taught Jennifer many things about what she did not want to do. It also taught her a great deal of compassion for how frozen one can become due to life's circumstances. Jennifer is grateful for that life because it is not a life that she ever wishes to repeat. Sometimes, the way you learn your "yes" is by first experiencing your "no."

There Is Only Now

There is a liminal moment before any birth, a moment of anticipation and realization that something is coming. The challenge is that when you focus on the future, constantly imagining what will come, you anticipate rather than experience. If you hope to connect with your deepest level of trust, it is crucial to shift away from a many-thousand-year-old model of forecasting: projecting, imagining, and troubleshooting the future. Instead, tune in to the spark that is already growing within you and feel that power. Connect to the Sacred Heart of Love within your body. You are made to create. You are instruments of the divine capable of manifesting your sacred destiny. You are procreative. Even if you never give birth to children, even if that is not your path, within you are seeds. Within your human nature, your DNA carries the codes of what you can become. It is already there.

You will die one day and transcend into another body. You will be born into another life and another experience. Your soul's journey is an evolution over many lifetimes. It is a process. So even if it feels like you have missed the mark, like you have had so many dreams and hopes that didn't quite get there, remember: this is a journey that is substantially longer than your individual human mind can comprehend. Instead of always looking forward to the future, connect to the spark of life that already exists within you so that you may deeply and completely access trust.

Eliminating the word "want" from your vocabulary is a key to this. "Want" holds you back because "to want" literally means "to lack." Any time you focus on "want," you go into a state of craving. To want means you do not have it yet. Want amplifies lack. It is a word encoded with a current absence of what you seek. Want, by its very nature, implies that the only time you might ever have it will be in the future, but your goal or resource is not here now. The paradox is that there is only now. Want is a can of wishes that gets kicked down the road towards a perpetual future. Conversely, when you tune into your desire and lean into the urge that pulls you towards hopeful possibilities, the universe offers glimmers of what can be. To manifest your heart's desire, embrace the gratitude, pleasure, and sense of enoughness within yourself in this very moment. That is a seed that may start very small, but it is the only seed that can grow.

Perhaps at the very beginning, as you start on this path, all you have time for is 60 seconds in the bathroom with a lit candle to utter a brief prayer while your toddler is distracted in the other room watching cartoons. It may be that you take a five-minute break outdoors between shifts bagging groceries. Moments of connection and peace may feel fleeting and temporary. Even if all you can carve out is 60 seconds, five minutes, maybe an hour a week, this is where you start. By turning to what feels good in your body, to what you are grateful for, to your delight, pleasure, and joy, you cultivate and amplify those qualities.

Now, if you have explored the Laws of Attraction, studied metaphysics, or spent time in the world of magic, then you probably know that where you direct your attention is what you amplify. Because of the way human beings need order and seek patterns to make meaning, you will collect evidence to confirm that what you believe about the world is true. What you focus on grows. So when you focus on wanting what you lack and fretting over the things that are not happening, we guarantee that this is what will continue.

To allow yourself to shift gears, give yourself permission to welcome pleasure. Grant yourself space to acknowledge what your actual predilections are. Claim your true, weird, deepest, heart-felt desires. Conversely, acknowledge the things that don't light you up. Sometimes you may be required to do those things, but there will be other times when you get to say "no."

We invite you to tune in to your truth. Start by creating a bold, audacious affirmation that reflects your desire. Speak the words aloud to yourself. Then, listen for what comes back. Experiment by saying, *"I deserve pleasure."* What do you immediately notice? Is there an easy, unbridled "yes?" Is there a "maybe" or some ambivalence? Or is there some part of you that resists and pushes back?

If you strongly feel, "Yes, I deserve pleasure," without hesitation, go you! You are further along in the game than many. Perhaps, though, you notice that a part of you replies back with something like "I don't know if I deserve pleasure. There are too many starving children in the world. There are too many people dying needlessly from violence, disease, and human stupidity. With all the misery in the world, who am I to feel pleasure? I deserve pleasure only if I earn it. Maybe when I complete XYZ, then I'll be worthy of pleasure." All of these conditions that arise are obstacles to address and clear so that you can invite, welcome, and embrace pleasure.

Healing issues can feel like you are peeling away the layers of an onion. What you initially imagined to be your challenges will morph to reveal more entrenched issues. Family agreements passed along for generations, inherited trauma, past life events, difficult memories from this life, and harmful conclusions may come to light. Persistence and thoroughness are the keys to successful healing. In some cases, it might be a memory of being reprimanded at the age of five when you asked for a second piece of birthday cake. In others, it was the message you repeatedly heard and witnessed playing out in your family that nice people don't make waves by asking for more than they're offered. Perhaps it unfolds into some deeply ingrained social programming.

For many, the idea of embracing pleasure brings up patriarchal conditioning about the archetype of the wanton, insatiable slut or spoiled brat. Who is she for you? The Haughty Princess? The Entitled Rich Girl? The Jezebel?

PERMISSION, DESIRE, & CREATIVE EXPRESSION

Pleasure starts with being here, right now, in this moment. Pleasure is about being embodied and embracing your desire. Will you plant a staff firmly in the ground like the wizard Gandalf and let your power radiate outward? Will you firmly declare, "You shall not pass! You shall not interfere with my pleasure or delight!" Granting yourself permission is a powerful way to initiate a shift.

Let's affirm some permissions. Place both hands over your heart and deliberately repeat the following statements.

"I give myself permission to pursue joy first.

I give myself permission to experience pleasure.

I give myself permission to let this be easy.

I give myself permission to embrace small delights every day.

I give myself permission to trust my own truth.

I give myself permission to recognize my limits and set boundaries.

I give myself permission to claim my 'yes' and assert my 'no.'

I am a cell in the body of this earth. I am a child of Divine Source. I am the embodiment of God/dess, and I claim my birthright to ease, flow, grace, bliss, passion, wonder, ecstasy, joy, and delight.

My moment is now. I declare my wholeness, enoughness, and worth, right here and right now."

Take a deep breath. How are you feeling? What shifts are you noticing? What feels possible now?

We urge you to retrieve, reclaim, and say "yes" to your deepest desires and stand up for what is meant to be yours. This facilitates the process that activates your bliss. Even if, at times, you are misperceived or feel invisible, as long as you genuinely know and trust yourself, who really cares? Within every single one of you, there is a creator. Within every single one of you dwells a unique purpose meant just for you. Though it may have been suppressed and squelched so early you can hardly remember it, it is still part of you. By the very nature of your aliveness and embodiment, you are creative. You come to a deeper state of trust, empowerment, ease, joy, and pleasure through following the creative urges within you.

While creativity may appear as you imagine, it can also be completely different than you expect. Creativity goes beyond writing a book, painting a masterpiece, composing a symphony, coding a life-changing piece of software, choreographing a dance performance, designing a bridge, or sculpting a replica of the Taj Mahal entirely out of white chocolate. Creativity can be going for a walk, noticing the beauty around you, and taking a couple of pictures. Creativity may be the way that you arrange food on a plate. It may be how you wander through a garden and select a bouquet of flowers. For some, dressing up is their way of being creative. For some, it is doing their hair and putting on their makeup. It may be the playlist you mix for a dear friend. It may be choosing a card at a gift store and expressing your love with a message of gratitude inside it. It may be a ridiculous pun that comes to your mind. It may be how you play with children.

Creativity is about following the innate part of you that's driven by an urge to express or make. Creativity unfolds from your passion to engage with whatever brings you delight and joy. There are so many different ways for it to manifest.

What do you love to do?

How do you play when no one is watching?

What are your hobbies?

What are the things that bring out your joy?

How are you creative?

Magic unfolds from knowing and embracing your heart's desire and acting upon it. The best way to anchor trust in yourself and the universe is to take inspired action with your creative urges. Move forward from your inner guidance and longings. Follow the breadcrumbs, the glimmers of light, the sparkle. Follow your joy and pursue the actions you are called to take. Commit to persistent, consistent, incremental effort. Allow yourself to be open to best possible outcomes. As you witness your capacity to manifest your dream – from the tiniest spark of inspiration to the initial and subsequent steps to the full realization of your desire – your confidence, hope, and trust are activated.

A big part of what you are here to do is to claim your power and integrate your truth. This is evident when you can honestly say:

> *"I embrace my life. I trust myself. I choose what is aligned. I claim my true desires, and I release everything that is mis-aligned for me. I choose my delight. I choose my pleasure. I say 'yes' to my body, and I claim truth, power, and creativity on my own terms."*

CHAPTER 3

THE WILL: SOVEREIGNTY

You humans are so afraid of your power. Your challenge is not your powerlessness, your vulnerability, or your weakness. That is an illusion. Your challenge is that you inhibit, suppress, and deny the truth of who you are. You eke by while shouldering boulders of fear, doubt and insecurity. What you are capable of is so much greater than what you allow yourselves. Yes, for many millennia, you have had limitations that prevented you from accessing your power. There has been scarcity. There have been shortages. These have inhibited your ability to grow. But we have given you tools, healing techniques, and sustainable technology. We have given you everything you need to live in abundance. We have given all of it to you, and yet you still play small.

YOUR ROLE IN THE WORLD

You are all profoundly interconnected. Many of you are coming to recognize yourselves as cells in the body of the earth. However, it is also important to claim your sovereignty and to recognize that you are distinct from anybody or anything else. This is the great paradox. You are part of us, you are one with us, and you are interconnected to all things. Yet, when you do not know yourself, and you cannot recognize what is yours and what is not yours, you cannot access your sovereignty. You cannot follow your own true will because you make choices that are based on the need to please, to fit in, and to be liked. What is called for at this point in time is separation from rules, expectations, social agreements, and legacies of limitation and lack. The global pandemic has been a dress rehearsal for you to choose your truth and your sovereignty. It has also been a culling of your social networks. This informed your choices about who you felt obliged to spend time with versus who you actually desired to spend time with. You are interconnected and part of something substantially greater than yourselves, but this requires that you are also able to go into stillness, aloneness – all-one-ness – so you may find your truth, sovereignty, and grace.

We wish to speak about how your beliefs and sense of identity influence the ways you compromise your sovereignty and relinquish your peace. Jennifer and her students have been examining their identities as highly sensitive people, empaths, and souls called to be of service on this planet. They've been exploring how they take on and absorb the misery of the world. When you believe that it is your responsibility to alleviate global suffering, often you are hobbled by that suffering. In your attempt to mitigate, help, and support, you extend your energy beyond your own sphere of influence. While every one of you has the agency to take action, make changes, and offer support, your human-centric perspective is disproportionate to your actual place in the family of things. Many of you believe that if you can feel it, it becomes your job to heal it. The irony is, when you feel it and thus attempt to heal it, you often deprive the actual actors of doing their own work – the work of feeling for themselves, experiencing and taking responsibility for the choices, actions, and consequences of their behavior. While it may appear at first glance that your sense of responsibility for the pain and suffering of others is only about service, it often creates a hindrance to the universe unfolding as it should because you have stepped beyond your own boundaries and responsibilities.

The first step to making changes is to comprehend what you believe about your role on this earth.

What do you think your responsibility is?

What do you imagine your job is?

To what extent do you feel compelled to interfere, intercede, or step beyond your own domain?

As long as you have operational beliefs that tell you it is your responsibility to absorb, feel, and process the pain of the world, you will be caught in a perpetual cycle of taking on the suffering of others, recognizing that you have done this, and then working to release it. The solution lies in breaking the rules, roles, and identities that you have adopted about what it means to be an empath. Consider why you believe that you need to extend your empathic sensitivity to absorb misery. You need to understand that while your desire is to be of help, when you take on external distress, you amplify it. You do not help at all. You pull the focus away from where the attention is needed.

Put your oxygen mask on your own face first.

Eliminate your need to take inventory, assess, and release the pain outside of yourself. Rescuing the world is not your job. Your job is to maintain peace within your own nervous system and to become a beacon for calm in the midst of the storm.

Before you find the core of peace within yourself, many of you, for countless reasons (including the belief that extending your energy beyond yourself is the way to gauge safety), lose your center. We will give you an image to work with. Jennifer recently noticed herself vacillating between states of peace and grace and states of agitation, confusion, and an urge to fix problems that are substantially greater than herself. As she tuned in to her core, she noticed that while there was a star of light within her own heart, she had extended many tendrils of inquiry outside herself and beyond her own boundaries. So that she could know what was going on in the world (and, theoretically, to protect herself), Jennifer had extended her energy field out like a set of tentacles, each one drawing in separate bits of information, energy, and chaos. She discovered that, although she was attempting to protect herself by gathering this information, she had gone beyond simply observing to actively absorbing the terror, despair, and grief of the world. What she drew in distorted her entire energy system. Instead of acting as a beacon to radiate calm, love, and healing, she had become increasingly anxious, distressed, and doubtful about her capacity to make a difference.

We worked with her to grasp how far outside of herself she had extended her energy. We helped her to recognize how her sense of identity and the rules she had created for herself (or agreed to) were driving this distress. This included rules handed down by her ancestors and society, as well as agreements and contracts formed through other lives, which came with her into this one. She began to understand. We asked her to examine and acknowledge how her identity as an empath caused her to believe she was responsible for feeling more than was hers. We encouraged her to scrutinize the ways she did this and to examine why she felt the need to extend her energy system. We showed her how, by absorbing external energy in the way that she does, she becomes debilitated. She is no longer effective. We showed her that, in the cosmic soup that comprises everything, there are streams of chaos and despair and streams of grace, ease, and love.

Like a number of you who are reading or listening to this book, Jennifer is one who, at this moment, lives in a safe and peaceful region on your planet. Extending her feelers out into areas of chaos, violence, and conflict changes her frequency from one of peace to one of agitation. When anyone in a pocket of peace absorbs the pain and havoc of another part of the world, it transforms their frequency. They were born to transmute, transform, and transmit peace, but they amplify distress instead.

This amplification begins as an inner experience. It shows up as emotional unease, mental perseveration, and a nagging sense that something is wrong. However, as time moves forward and you continue to take on more negativity, it will manifest on a physical level. This could be in the form of sickness, disaster, accident, or untimely death. A frequency of peace will create more peace in the world. A frequency of distress will only magnify distress. We showed Jennifer her place in the river of life. We imparted how she is a glimmer flowing in a stream of peace within this universe. This is her role. It is the role given to many of you -- to be a glimmer in a stream of peace. We also showed how fragile that stream can be. When she extends her tendrils into areas of agony and desperation, she absorbs the misery and feels fear as a result. Her frequency, which is meant to generate love and tranquility, ceases to broadcast grace and intensifies fear and despair instead.

CALLING YOURSELF HOME

At this point in time, it is imperative that you protect and maintain your peace. This means you *do not* extend your energy out into the world so you can absorb the thoughts, feelings, and energy around you in an attempt to make yourself safe. Trust that you can be aware of what is happening without having to either feel it or heal it. Your peace is essential. It is needed above all things right now. Tranquility is how you will be able to navigate this time of great transformation, upheaval, and transition.

Before you can truly and completely sustain your peace, you must call in all the parts of yourself that have jumped the fence, the aspects of yourself that are now hurtling around the universe trying to make sense of things. Return to your soul center. Return to your heart.

> To that end, we invite you to join us in a meditation.
>
> It is time to call in all parts of yourself and return to your soul's center.
>
> Examine whether there is a part of you that has extended your energy beyond your own domain. Have you cast feelers out to the people, places, or things that have you troubled?
>
> Return to your own heart center. Remember, at the very core of all of your concern and despair is love. This is the desire to be of service and your longing to be restored to grace. As you become aware of how and what you have taken on, we entreat you to

acknowledge and honor your grief. Grief for lives lost, grief for what seems uncontrollable and inconsolable. Let yourself feel that grief. Sink into the love that holds it, because without love, grief would not exist.

Grief is always an expression of love.

Return to your heart. Cultivate love. Send it to every concern. Let it ripple beyond you. Let it spread until it reaches the places of rage, chaos, and turbulence.

As you breathe in, breathe love into your heart. Let it strengthen and grow. Then, exhale and radiate love to everywhere that needs it most.

Allow the light of love to transmute all of your feelers. Extend that love through yourself and outward until all of the hopelessness, terror, and confusion has been transmuted into loving acceptance. Allow it to be transfigured into pure light.

As you broadcast love, all that you have absorbed recalibrates. As you draw back those tendrils, the fear disintegrates. Allow your cords to return to you. Breathe your light back in. Love can only be amplified. It both remains where you send it and returns to you magnified.

Repeat after us: "I radiate kindness through my cords as they transmute into pure light. I send love to all pain and suffering, both within and without me. I choose love and release all energy that is not mine. I flood all my connections with mercy and compassion. I inhale love and exhale it out. I call myself home. I reel my cords of light back to me."

Allow yourself to float in the river of peace. Become a beacon of calm. Allow yourself to become the frequency of peace amplified into the universe.

And so it is.

The reason it is so important to maintain this frequency of peace is that when you are in a state of grace and peace, you are able to respond instead of react. When you respond rather than react, you can accomplish things for which you have no capacity when you are triggered, fearful, or distressed. So, while some might say that cultivating peace and love or sending thoughts and prayers are just frivolous actions, we would say that nothing could be further from the truth!

To access your sovereignty, you must claim space for yourself. Claim time away from distractions. Step away from all of the external influences and obligations. Sometimes, that can only happen one minute at a time. Step away. Unplug completely for that minute. Regroup. It may be as simple as going into another room and putting one hand over your heart, one hand on your navel, and simply breathing into your body again, saying:

I breathe in my truth. I breathe in my strength. I breathe into myself. I choose me. I give myself permission to make myself the priority.

There is such a paradox in your sovereignty because your sovereignty is only defined by your relationship to other beings, other things, and other situations. When you are by yourself, your sovereignty is not an issue. You only become conscious of it in relation to others. It is through this contrast that you can discern whether you are compromising or in alignment with your "yes" or "no." To access your sovereignty and the truth of your "yes" and "no," taking space is vital. Step away from all of the influences that distract you, pull on you, or harry you. Otherwise, you will not be in alignment with divine grace and embodying a power substantially greater than yourself. When the ego runs your will, you express your power from limitation, strain, and conflict.

True boundaries and true sovereignty contain a firm grace that allows you to simply state what is and follow your divine path. You move in the direction you are supposed to go. Ego-driven power is not real power. More often than not, you are reacting to what you do *not* want. You find yourself fighting and pushing away, as opposed to calling in your true desire. When you are in true sovereignty, you know your path. You know your "yes," and you know where you are going. You become so focused on the direction you need to go that there is no room for opposition. This can only happen when you step away from the socialization, expectations, and obligations that inhibit you. All the things that keep you playing small – worrying about what other people think, your weight, how you will pay the next bill, and the behavior of others – stop you in your tracks.

To release patterns that no longer serve you, cease to perceive human romance as the be-all and end-all of your needs. Recognize that the human relationship is a mirror of your relationship with the divine. All human relationships are designed to reflect

Sacred Union. When you are in full alignment, the receptive, intuitive, inner part of yourself informs the physical, embodied, outer part of you that takes action in the world.

For millennia, you have allowed the material world to define and direct the show. As a result, the physical has called the shots and demanded what it wants. The emotional and intuitive have tried desperately to meet the needs of the physical from a deficit. The inner has looked to the outer instead of the divine for guidance and inspiration. As a result, you humans have lost your way. You have forgotten who and what you are. You have lost your head. Because *we* are your head.

We are the way. We are your consciousness. We are the mainframe. We deliver the information to you. You are the processor that parses the information – the information that is relevant to you in your current incarnation.

For millennia, many of your kind have been disconnected and separated from us. You have allowed a small handful of authorized spokespeople to speak on our behalf. Often, they transmitted their own beliefs, which were not necessarily our truths. You have been approaching things in reverse order. You have been going at it from the external. You have started from the bottom of the funnel instead of the top. This has led to fretting, which triggers emotional woes and impulsive reactions. This is the complete opposite of how we wish you to do this.

THE END OF SEPARATION: AN INSIDE JOB

The last 10,000 years have acted as a retrograde period for your planet. This has been an experiment. You have learned by playing with duality. You have embraced scenarios such as succumbing to scarcity. You have ruminated over questions like, "What will happen if everything falls into the void? What will happen if we flip a switch and turn the whole world upside down? What if we turn the fan backward? What if we reach for the flame?" You have learned a great deal from this experiment of disconnection and separation.

Before this retrograde period, you were simply of the earth and had no sense of ego or individuality. You were informed, connected, and motivated by instinct alone. In order for your consciousness to evolve as a species, as an entire living entity, you have had to experience this separation, externalization, and a sense of moving away from the collective. It is only through the contrast created by this experiment that you are able to recognize the price of separation. This is what Abrahamic religions (Judaism, Christianity, and Islam) refer to as the Fall from Grace and the Exile from Paradise.

Before, you were as little children who innocently experienced the bliss of mother's milk. You were a nursing babe. You accepted her love and succor. You could trust, knowing you were nestled in Earth's bosom. You were loved and supported, but you did not know what you were. You did not understand yourself. You were unaware of your own magnitude. As I Am That I Am, you are that you are because you are Me. To fully actualize the magnificence of what is possible as a being on this earth, you needed a period of separation. That period is now coming to an end.

The earth has been in retrograde and is now getting ready to go direct. Awakened empaths perceive this. The return of the comet NEOWISE was a sign that you are coming out of this retrograde. To free yourself of limitations to your sovereignty, let go of the outdated perception that you need to change the outside world first. Instead, embrace the understanding that only through changing your internal landscape can you actually make changes in the outer world. As Earth goes direct, you can facilitate this release of the old by realigning your focus away from external reality as defining your happiness. You have let your jobs define your fulfillment and become your raison d'etre. It is time to focus on cultivating inner peace and the expression of love from your heart. Cease to submit to the bidding of ego. Learn to focus on your inner well-being instead of looking for external fulfillment.

Many of the humans controlling the planet right now are not even being run by their ego; they are being run by their id. They react from their toddler selves because of the trauma that they endured. This highlights the way this retrograde has heightened your collective sense of separation. Many of you find yourselves caught in the trap of reacting to the wounded ids of hotheads. The dictators and fascists are not so much catalysts as they are the manifestation of your collective wounds. You resonate with them, either positively or negatively, because you are carrying this distortion in your field. You have been functioning from a space of, "I've got to put that fire out," as opposed to, "I will find my calm center, then I will evaluate and respond." Yes, you need to move quickly to put out a fire, but there is a difference between extinguishing it from panic and anxiety and doing so from centeredness.

Many years ago, when Jennifer used to attend fire circle gather-ings, she got to the point where she was so in alignment that she could walk within six inches of a fire that was almost as tall as she was. She could reach her hand in, grab a smoldering log, flip it around, and place it. She was able to tend the fire in a way that she never got burned. She was able to ask the smoke to work with her, so she wasn't inhaling it. She was in communion with the flame, and the fire was gracious. You spend so much time thinking that the elements and the earth are unconscious, that the earth is not listening to you and does not want to work in your favor. Instead of negotiating with fire, water, air, and earth, you react with panic to the wildfires, droughts, floods, hurricanes, tornadoes, and earthquakes. These disasters are symptoms of how out of balance you have become collectively.

As you are reading or listening to this, you may be thinking, "But this is so much bigger than I am! How is changing my energy going to fix this? There are forest fires all over the globe. There are floods consuming entire regions. How can my energy and effort make a difference?" What we will say is that this is an incremental shift. It has to begin with somebody. You, empath, are one of the people who are being called to make the incremental shift. As an empath, you not only have the ability to be a receiver who picks up all of the thoughts, feelings, energy, and sensations of the world around you, but you also have the capacity to be a broadcaster who transmits a signal of balance out into the world so it can shift. You are experiencing this distress because you have the capacity to make a difference. This starts with you. This starts with claiming space for yourself and learning to flip the current from an external focus to a divine focus that comes from a source far greater than you. It enters your heart and blossoms into guidance. It manifests as the part of you that knows. That part guides and leads your body to take action. This is how you need to shift the way you are living in the world.

Know this: by the fact that you are a cell in the body of the earth, you are sovereign. Regardless of whether you are human, furred, feathered, scaled, leafed, or mineral, you are sovereign, and your sovereignty is no greater or less than anyone else's. The way you engage with others can become an invitation rather than the obligation to which society has conditioned you.

You can perceive this through your dynamics with power structures and the distinction between collaboration and dominance. To establish and maintain sovereignty, set effective boundaries, recognize your "yes," and claim your "no," you must shift away from force and dictatorship. It is time for hierarchies and pecking orders to become obsolete. This starts as an inside job. Power over only works because you consent to either subordinate or impose your will upon others. When you cease to participate on either side of this equation, you cease to fuel this archaic system.

NOTHING LEFT TO LOSE

For many, society demonstrated the use of force as a means to express power and set limits. You were led to believe that if you merely requested something, you would not receive it. You'd immediately anticipate the "no." You'd need to fight for any gain, and this would be at the expense of others. You'd set boundaries and define your needs based on what you did not want and with the anticipation of conflict. You'd gird your loins, pump up your moxie, and rally your fierceness. You'd summon your inner warrior for the fight. As opposed to a mutually beneficial negotiation, you'd approach boundaries as a preparation for battle. Even now, so many define their terms from "no" instead of "yes." However, you are beginning to transcend fighting for what you do not want. We invite you to experiment by declaring, "This is what I desire. This is what excites me. This is what I imagine might be possible. Would you like to join me?" How would it feel to move towards what you long for, as opposed to away from what you do not? Tuning in to desire is the key to establishing and protecting true sovereignty.

Numerous humans have jobs at which they're wholly adequate, they make a decent income, and they find their situations tolerable. Unfortunately, many humans are employed at jobs they barely endure or absolutely loathe. Work and earning money are beyond drudgery. They experience it through a vale of tears. And yes, it is awful. The irony is that as long as they focus on how awful it is, they deprive themselves of the pursuit of things they love, enjoy, and deserve.

You can certainly turn toward your sense of obligation, burden, and responsibility. Conversely, you can also turn toward pleasure, what you truly desire, and what you are called to do. Even if this means that for the time being you are washing dishes, bagging groceries, pushing gurneys in an emergency room, or being employed by a corporation that makes you feel like your soul is being sucked out of your body, you still get to stand in your sovereignty. In every single moment, you can turn toward your joy, or you can turn toward despair. There are many things you do have a choice about, but because your species has been externally focused for so long, you define your agency by your circumstances.

We urge you to cease focusing on what you cannot do and start turning your focus towards what you can do. For millennia, your attention has been directed at the negative, on what you detest and what needs fixing. Claim your power. Flip the switch. Focus on what you love and embrace your agency and the self-advocacy available to you at any given moment. You always have choices. You choose whether you go outside and look up at the sky with a sense of gratitude and wonder or you look down at the cracked pavement and tell yourself that your life sucks. You get to decide whether you will spend that hour of time before you go to sleep catching up on current events or writing in your journal. You get to decide whether you drink water or tea. These are things you can control. These are choices you get to make.

At first, these minor options might feel like the only things you have control over. They may appear to be the few areas of life where you have a choice. To create a life you long for, it is imperative that you own your choice and take action in all areas where you have agency, self-advocacy, and control. To begin with, identify where you actually have control. Will you respond to that incendiary message, or will you leave it to marinate? What music will you listen to as you travel? What color underwear would you like to wear? Which flavor of salad dressing will you purchase? What will you say to that stranger?

We now offer a brief exercise. Set aside 15 to 30 minutes and grab a journal or piece of paper. At the top of the page, write the words *"I Could Never"* on the left side and *"I Have To"* on the right side. In the first column, jot down everything you believe you could never do. "I could never abandon my family. I could never make a living as an artist. I could never tell my friend how I really felt. I could never ..." You fill it in. In the second column, write everything you feel obligated to do. "I have to stay married until my kids are grown. I have to visit my mother in the nursing home every week. I have to keep my job for the health insurance." Notice how many external things you bind yourself to out of doubt, fear, and a sense of obligation.

Initially, emancipation from all the "shoulds" will be tiny and incremental. It may start with what flavor of toothpaste you choose. However, as you begin to empower yourself through minor choices, you open to the possibility to claim more space and time for yourself. Thus, your sovereignty expands within you. Subsequently, as part of the body of the earth, your sovereignty expands beyond your individuality.

This is not about becoming a leader who sits in their ivory tower watching and issuing orders. Instead of thinking of yourself as a monarch who exerts power over your dominion, what if you thought of yourself as one who holds the vision and conducts its unfolding?

We must stress the distinction between sovereignty and willfulness. What many of you have perceived as sovereignty in your culture is actually willfulness. Willfulness manifests as attempts to control, manipulate, and force your agenda. This places competitive supremacy over mutually beneficial empowerment. It is key to be sovereign, but it is also essential to be in relation. True sovereignty takes the well-being of everyone and everything into consideration. Inspired by divine connection, you see the sparks and follow the trail of light. From there, you share your insight and vision with the world. Perhaps you welcome others to join you. Some will have received a similar call. They behold the spark and discern what's aligned. And, because they are sovereign too, they choose what works best for them. Perhaps the one person you sincerely wish would become involved is not the one who says "yes." This is where you learn to trust the unfolding of the universe. Instead of your chosen person begrudgingly accepting your misaligned invitation, divinely aligned and perfect people will embrace the mission.

Humans are evolving away from power over dominion. You are moving away from the idea of giving orders and expecting people to respond to them, or conversely, being ordered and feeling obliged to act. You are being invited to join an interconnected, co-created experience of your universe. Sometimes, it will be a great party. Sometimes, there may only be one or two people who come along for the ride. Sometimes, you will be on your own with this because it is your personal mission. Ironically, what many of you think is a solo job is a mission many have been called to. Because you think you are alone with the magnitude of it, you are frightened. This is exacerbated by doubt, insecurity, and a fear of persecution that has been amplified since the crucifixion of Jesus.

Human bodies – your physical form of cells, tissues, organs, and systems – carry the visceral trauma of the crucifixions, the burning times, the wars, the genocides, the ages of slavery, and all the other ways your species has scourged and tortured itself. You carry dread for how you were annihilated because you spoke your truth, stepped up, and put yourself out into the world. As a result, even though there is a vast collective of beings who are receiving similar downloads, visions, and guidance, many of you are paralyzed by the fear of being annihilated again. As we have told you, you are immortal. You cannot be annihilated. Yes, your body will die. Your body may even have to endure severe agony and pain. Your soul will have to shake it off. It is likely that you will have to do some work between incarnations (maybe well into your next lives) as you process the impact of a challenging death. But there is so much more than that. All is well on the other side. Once you cross over, you will enter the golden lands of bliss. Perhaps we might say, "No harm, no foul."

You and many others are being called to coalesce and support the realization of a New Earth. Because your planet is at such a point of precariousness, you have everything to lose as humans but nothing to lose as immortal souls. It is time to play all in. It is time to recognize who you are. It is time to send your signal out to the world. It is time to enlist your collaborators to join you in this work. We suggest you imagine there is nothing left to lose.

Your Heart Is The Way

Many of you feel our call and follow the inspiration we've given you, yet many do this through the lens of ego. You do it with the belief that you are the sole creator and the inspiration is yours alone. None of this is yours alone! We are seeding consciousness and awareness across the planet right now. We plant these seeds of knowledge in many of you.

There is a new wave of channeled material, guidance, and information being shared with your world right now. It comes in the form of books, speeches, poetry, art, music, light language transmissions, and more. We offer our messages in a myriad of ways. We hedge our bets by speaking through many different channels. Different people align to different songs and unique frequencies. It is all music. It is all our music. Each channel sings or expresses it in different ways to reach you most effectively. Some people will read or hear Jennifer's transmission and understand the way she expresses us. Her particular way of sharing our message will resonate in ways that other channels do not. Yet Jennifer is one of many who are doing this work. It is our hope that the information we share in this book will confirm your own guidance as well as reinforce messages you have received from additional sources. Our truth is expressed through many. Therefore, please know that anyone who claims sole authority or states they have proprietary rights to Divine Source is best encountered with scrutiny. Use your discernment. Do not grant them more authority than your own inner knowing just because they assert their message with confidence, authority, or bravado. We are Universal, and our wisdom is accessible and available to all of you.

To connect with us, you must *choose* us. Harness your thoughts to let them be tools for your intuition and your emotions. The path is not through intellect. It is found through inspiration and sincere feeling. The journey itself prompts your response or reaction. Ideas arise from your heart. Your thoughts are born of your feelings. The way that you find us, the way that you are able to express us, is always through your heart.

Your heart is the vehicle through which we manifest. Your vulnerability and open heart allow you to access our guidance. This is what forms the visions, thoughts, and ideas in your head. But before you can be a clear, open channel for us, you must regulate your emotions. Stabilize your nervous system. Learn how to be mindful of your feelings so you can respond instead of react. As long as you keep putting out fires, reacting to triggers, and immediately jumping to conclusions, you cannot access us to the full extent of what is possible. We encourage you to look at the crutches and self-soothing mechanisms you use. They cloud your judgment and emotional stability. They inhibit your ability to be honest with yourself. The first part of the journey to connection with us lies in your own emotional and mental recovery.

The next part of the journey is to experience what it is to simply be yourself. Start moving through the waters of your subconscious. From there, journey through the dreams, feelings, and experiences of being you. Once you surrender to inhabiting your heart, we will give you guidance. Eventually, this guidance will coalesce as thoughts. Instead of appearing as specific details or precise instructions such as "you need to buy an XYZ car," we will give you the frequency of what we wish for you. We give you a sense of it. We initiate your desire. Then, we lead you to it – one incremental action at a time.

We encourage you to stop trying to visualize concrete details. In the past, people created vision boards pasted with pictures of luxury cars, five-star accommodations, the sexy bodies they believed would improve their lives, clothing designed to elevate social status, and other symbols of outer wealth and success. Those vision boards of the 80s and 90s did serve you. However, they externalize your heart's desires. Consider them training wheels for the manifestation now possible. While lovely and completely acceptable, this focus on status and things substantially limits what you, as a human being, are capable of. So, we impart feelings. We will give you hints. We drop bread crumbs along your way. We give you little guideposts and confirmation chills. When necessary, we throw up a detour to move you in the direction you need to go. We also provide the instinct for when the right and aligned choice comes to you.

Here is an example of how this can work. Years ago, Jennifer and her husband dedicated their honeymoon to house hunting. They looked at countless properties online. They did drive-bys to check out listings. They explored numerous listings, but every single one of them was just a "maybe we could do this" or "yeah, no, absolutely not." It wasn't until they drove onto a particular piece of land that they knew they were home. As of the writing of this book, they have lived on this property for 22 years. As soon as they drove up the long dirt road to the house, their bodies felt the "yes." They knew this was the home they had been searching for. The "yes" was instant. This is the way we work. This is how you know when you are in alignment with us.

Here's another example. For a few months, we dropped hints about welcoming a new kitten into Jennifer's family. She had formed an image in her mind that it would be a little, all-gray, short-haired male. Every night, she pored over the rescue sites in search of this specific kitten. Then, one evening, she found "the kitten." The next day, she and her husband drove up to the Humane Society to adopt this 8-week-old baby. However, by the time they arrived, that kitten had already been adopted. Not only had he been adopted, but so had every other male kitten. But we encouraged her to check out a pair of tiny black females. Forty-five minutes later, they drove home with a kitten. She was not the kitten Jennifer imagined, but she was the kitten we had for her. Never has Jen experienced a sweeter, more agreeable cat than ZuZu. Within a week, she'd stolen everyone's hearts, including their curmudgeonly tuxedo cat, Livi. We instigated the desire. We provided the nudge Jen needed to go where she was meant to go. It was her willingness to surrender the details that allowed this connection to happen. Being able to recognize the aligned "yes" is a knowing that deepens. It starts first with doing the emotional work. Then, it evolves so you can access the hints and energetic and emotional frequencies we send to you. Eventually, it will become a seamless relationship of guidance between you and us.

BECOME YOUR OWN BELOVED

What we share next may be a bitter pill to swallow. To embody sovereignty, you must relinquish "romantic" love. Romantic love, as you currently define and experience it, is a lethal illusion that is killing you. You have been taught that this is the ultimate way to be satisfied and fulfilled. You have made romance your priority and placed sexual engagements over all other forms of intimacy. Romance has caused you to externalize your rescue. You have learned to believe that someone other than yourself is your savior and your medicine. To fully claim your sovereignty, redefine yourself as whole and complete unto yourself. Become a virgin again. Now, to be clear, we are not talking about never having sex. We are not talking about depriving yourself of pleasure and ecstatic bliss. We are talking about owning your power and taking actions based solely on what is ideal for your highest good rather than acting on what another human being can and will do for you. This does not have to mean that you will never get married. This does not have to mean that you will not have numerous beloveds in your life. You can have a life partner and still remain sovereign. The challenge arises when you look to another person to make you happy. Whenever you seek other people to fulfill your needs or feel incomplete because you do not have a romantic partner in your life, you throw your sovereignty out the window.

Become your own beloved. Become your own primary relationship. Marry yourself first. Dwell in communion with yourself. Be true and loyal to yourself. Trust yourself implicitly and be faithful. Fidelity starts with yourself, first and foremost. This is essential for you to evolve. As long as you continue to base your reality on bad television, romance novels, and glossy Hollywood movies, you will give away your power again and again. You will make choices that cannot serve you. Your path is found through clear guidance and sincere feelings. Take the action of claiming yourself, grounding yourself, and anointing yourself as sacred, beloved, and chosen.

As you start to engage with your power, will, and sovereignty, it is imperative that you also engage with discernment. This is especially pertinent as you begin to heal from triggers, traumas, and previous crises. When you carry old wounds, it is entirely possible that what you perceive as sovereignty and intuition is actually a reaction to old triggers. You need to comprehend the difference between reacting and responding. You need to recognize when you are running away from distress versus when you are following the urge toward joy, bliss, and delight.

If power has only been expressed through aggression and you have never experienced true sovereignty, then following your bliss will feel different and unfamiliar. First, you will need to evaluate it. We'll give you an example. When Jennifer was younger and learning to navigate her relationship with food (particularly with chocolate), she would have to pay attention, tune in, and ask herself, "Do I actually desire this, or am I craving it because I'm feeling a lack or a need? Am I feeling out of sorts and trying to fill a hole, or will this bring me true delight?" Discernment invites you to distinguish between want and desire. The questions to ask yourself as you follow the sovereign path are, "Do I want this, or do I actually desire this? Am I reacting, or am I responding?"

Humans make desire so complicated. The problem is that you have not experienced unmitigated desire in eons. Your species has experienced urgency, hunger, need, and want for so long that you have stopped being able to recognize what your true desire is. Desire does not have urgency. Desire does not clutch. Desire is an inkling, an idea, a sense of possibility like, "Hmm, what would happen if I went down this path?" It does not have the desperation of want. True desire is something you know with your whole being. You feel a complete "yes" to it in your body. Simultaneously, there is a calmness and a detachment to it. You can let go of the outcome because you trust that this or something better is manifesting in your life.

THE IMPACT OF TRAUMA

We need to talk about what it looks like to react to your triggers. Jennifer recalls a person whose childhood was ghastly. Even before birth, their biological mother experienced tremendous upheaval. During childhood they endured incredible amounts of neglect, abuse, and rejection. Their young adulthood was difficult as well. It was rife with bouts of alcoholism, family drama, and struggles trying to fit in as a gay and gender-fluid person. Despite all of this, they are determined, courageous, and willing. They have done an incredible amount of work to reclaim their power and autonomy. However, they still carry the impact of their trauma in their body and mind. Frequently, when they experience inconveniences, conflicts, or power struggles, their young, wounded inner child forms conclusions and interprets the encounter. They feel slighted, targeted, and insulted. Whatever the challenge, they regard it as evidence that people mean them harm. Activated by the current encounter, they switch from a calm adult capable of agency and advocacy to a fierce, battle-ax-wielding ogre whose sole purpose is to protect and defend the terrified child within. Their rational, grown-up part is overridden by the hurt toddler who runs the emotional show. Their frustration and resentment are often understandable and justified, but their reaction is disproportionately intense in relation to the current event. The conclusions they form about their present circumstance are clouded by their earlier trauma. The inner child, who has commandeered the nuclear codes, creates the narrative. They extrapolate details from childhood and conflate painful experiences of the past with their situation now.

You all have inner children. They are the source of your play and creativity. The inner child is the part of you that can access pure, unhampered emotions. They are capable of enormous joy and monumental despair. Your inner child lets you know when something is out of alignment or off balance. This part gets scared, angry, sad, and even has total meltdowns to alert you of real or imagined danger, challenges, and the need for change. This is completely normal and appropriate. The problem arises when that child is given the keys to the ignition and allowed to drive the bus. You all have times when you become emotionally dysregulated. You all have parts of yourselves that cannot be sovereign over your emotions. This happens to everyone at times. When your adult is able to recognize that you have moved into the fight, flight, freeze, or fawn mode, you retain your agency. Unfortunately, because few have learned how to effectively clear trapped triggers, many can not maintain mindfulness in stressful situations.

Proportionately few people have done much inner child work. Until recently, survival has taken precedence over introspection and emotional healing. While more of you are discovering how to heal, a large majority of humanity does not have the knowledge, tools, or willingness to clear their traumatic wounds. Many of you have not healed the wounds you still carry from childhood. Sadly, many were taught that their trauma is irrevocable. Memories would haunt them forever, and they'd have to struggle through life in the face of unresolved trauma. Fortunately, you now have resources and techniques that can allow you to heal.

In addition to your own trauma, you also contain wounds that you carry from your ancestral lines. Just think for a moment how many people came before you and endured hardships and struggles. Every generation you go back, the number doubles. From two parents and four grandparents, you move to eight great-grandparents. By the time you reach ten generations, you have 1,024 ancestors whose trials, tribulations, beliefs, and unresolved legacies are carried in your ancestral lines. By the time you go back twenty generations, the number has increased to over one million individuals, and there are merely 500 years between now and then. Go back thirty generations to around the thirteenth century, and the number of your ancestors is over one billion. In less than a thousand years, you have more ancestors than people who walked the earth; this number is more than double the world's population at that time.

The magnitude of this is almost incomprehensible and means at least two things. First, when you go back far enough in your genealogy, you are all related to each other. Second, your ancestors from 30 generations back contribute to multiple lines in your family tree. Not only have you inherited trauma from your parents, your grandparents, and your great-grandparents, it goes all the way back to your origins. When you consider the gravity of all that you carry, it is completely understandable why so often you have inner five-year-olds trying to drive the bus and control the situation.

Here is the paradox: the impact of all this inherited trauma has caused you to view yourselves as separate and isolated. When you perceive yourself as an individual being, you may fear that turning your life and will over to Divine Source is synonymous with giving away your autonomy. You imagine that if you surrender to something greater than yourself, you will lose your freedom of choice.

When you persist in living from your isolated identity, you are tenuously connected to us. You are only functioning at 1% of what is possible for you. We suggest that when fear is behind the wheel, you are driving toward urgency, need, and addiction, not toward the aligned path of light.

We wish you to be sovereign with all your emotions. We'd like you to acknowledge your feelings. Only with this awareness can you allow yourself to find the right bus and go in the right direction. Only with mindfulness will you be where you belong, in divine order at the right time and in the right place.

In truth, we are you. You are part of us. We are the greater consciousness of all.

Let us take the wheel. Allow us to drive. Step across the passenger line and find your seat on the bus. Sit with those scared inner children and offer them comfort. We will get you where you need to go in a way that your inner five-year-old, 15-year-old, or 23-year-old never will. Your discernment unfolds from asking yourself the question, *"Who is driving this bus?"*

THE PROMISE OF TRUE SOVEREIGNTY

Time is not linear, and the future does not exist. All time and all space is an illusion. Everything is going on simultaneously. The only thing that exists is now. It is always now. Therefore, the fact that you are here in this moment means you exist eternally. While your form may shift and transmute, your essence remains constant. We hope that you can take comfort in this. We hope you might begin to grasp the vastness of the eternity that you are a part of. You disempower yourself whenever you make predictive statements about disasters and crises you fear might come to pass. Prophesy declared as truth poisons the well and contaminates your timelines. Perseverating takes that predictive statement six steps further. It is a form of awfulizing that will send you plummeting down the rabbit hole.

Lately, many humans have asserted "truths" about events yet to occur. They speak about situations as if they've already come to pass. For example, "Climate change is destroying our planet." While sadly, this is a trajectory your species is perilously close to realizing, it is not your current reality. A more empowered thing to say is, "I am heartbroken and devastated by the choices we human beings are making. I am terrified that if we don't change our behavior, the earth is going to experience a cataclysmic disaster." This way, you own your fear and grief instead of projecting it outside of yourself and declaring it as something that already is. This is something that, especially as a magical practitioner, we wish to caution you against. Do not speak the future as truth, ever. Do not speak the positive future as truth; do not speak the negative future as truth. Speak from your desire instead: "I pray to live on a planet where everyone is fed and sheltered, where there is plenty, where we recognize the abundance that we have, and where we are all doing our healing work."

It is more powerful to align with the truth of your emotions than to externalize them by expressing feelings as predictions.

Notice whenever you feel anger, fear, or despair and start to make a declarative statement such as, "Oh, my God! We are going to hell in a handbasket" or "This country is going down the tubes." We could offer more examples, but you get the point. Whenever you make those kinds of prognostications, you undermine yourself and, through the Laws of Attraction, you reinforce a reality that you do not want. Whenever you focus on the opposite of what you wish to move towards, you imagine and thus create a field of possibility for these things to manifest. You reinforce the potential by sharing your wretched forecast with others.

Once you take up fear and move into projection, you detach from present reality, you dissociate from emotion, and you disconnect from your power. You cease to be sovereign anymore. You will try to disassociate because it feels too painful to sit with the discomfort. To resist despair, you externalize your distress as a convincing story.

Sovereignty is about being willing to be willing to sit with all of your feelings. Sovereignty is about being present with yourself and letting your emotions flow. The paradox is that emotions flow when you allow them to, and often, just like weather, they shift rapidly. It is when you resist and get trapped in emotions about emotions that you amplify them and remain stuck. When you own your fear, grief, and rage, you honor your vulnerability and authentic humanness. This is how you access the source of your greatest power: your heart.

We invite all of you who are reading or listening to this book to commit to curbing your predictions and perseveration. Make the choice to notice when you have launched into awfulizing. Become mindful of when you make predictive statements and imagine one worst-case scenario after the next. Before you go any further with tales of dread and woe, put your hands over your heart and tune into what you are actually feeling. If you sense deep despair and sadness, acknowledge and own it: "I feel really sad that this happened. I feel really angry. I feel really scared."

It may not feel comfortable because sadness, anger, and fear are emotions that your species has been discouraged from feeling for ages. Only by owning, accepting, and embracing these feelings will you as a species become sick and tired of being sick and tired and choose something different. As long as you keep kicking the can down the road by projecting your despair, anger, and fear, you will not have agency, nor will you be in coherence with the impact of your collective choices. Only when you feel the effects can you respond to make different choices.

In the same way that you must allow an alcoholic wake up in their own vomit, humans have to face all the chickens that have come home to roost. You can turn the drunk on their side, put a blanket over them, and leave them to sleep it off, but if you drive them home, clean them up, and throw their intoxicated body in the shower so that they will not wake up in their own stink, they will not have to face the consequences of their choices. When you do not feel the consequences of your choice to project your despair, anger, and fear, you are not forced to change. Instead, you just keep delaying the inevitable.

The essential thing to do is to own your feelings and release other people's feelings back to them. One approach you might take, especially if you notice someone is awfulizing, is to reflect their emotions back to them: "Wow! That sounds hard. I can only imagine how scary that feels." "I imagine that feels incredibly sad." "That must feel totally enraging." This way, you help somebody recognize that they have feelings about a situation instead of continuing to project their emotions outside of themselves.

As you come more deeply into your sovereignty, you own your own feelings and let other people own theirs. Empaths may focus on other people's feelings to avoid experiencing their own. To genuinely master your sovereignty, you must become willing to own the depth of your heart. Become willing to hand other people's emotions back to them. It is not your job to feel their feelings for them. Nor, however, is it your job to encourage them to feel or accept their emotions. Your job is to simply recognize whenever you are picking up somebody else's thoughts, feelings, energy, and sensations and processing them as if they are your own. Claim your own feelings and release everything else.

The promise of true sovereignty is your magnificence unbound. It restores you to right relation with the divine so that you may live as children of the earth and sky and become channels for both. You are capable of receiving divine guidance, calibrating, and following your aligned path. Because you are embodied and of the earth, you are capable of acting upon her guidance. When you embrace your sovereignty, commit to the work, and own yourself on all levels – physical, mental, emotional, spiritual, and any other aspects of your existence – you achieve the realization of your true self. You become a radiant beacon on this planet, a lighthouse that beams with love, possibility, and grace. When other beings come into your frequency, it activates within them too. We invite you to join us and claim your sovereignty. Ignite the light within you. Embrace every facet of you, warts and all – the scary, messy, and fraught, as well as the love, light, and grace. Connect with us. Express your true, glorious self.

You deserve to shine.

CHAPTER 4

THE HEART: INTERCONNECTION

Grant yourself permission to feel how deeply interconnected you are to all things. Empathic stress will cause you to avoid this interconnection. You will pull away because part of you fears that if you truly feel your interconnection, you will drown in it. For you to become actualized, restored, and renewed, it is essential that you go to the well and drink from it. Be replenished by the Sacred Well of Light that is the Universal Heart of Love.

INDIVIDUALS WITHIN THE COLONY

All earthly beings are in the process of being restored, renewed, and replenished. The Universal Heart is your home, and your heart is the portal. You are collectively finding your way home. We are leading you to enter your heart and to recognize how profoundly interrelated you are to all things. Your heart is the means to retrieve awareness of yourselves as individual facets within a colony of many.

If you are a Star Trek fan, you are probably familiar with the Borg. This representation of the hive mind reveals the significant fear humans have of being assimilated into a collective consciousness. The Borg is a malevolent example. They assimilate and wipe out entire planets. You can find additional examples with classic vampire and werewolf tales, portrayals of the zombie apocalypse, and alien invasions. All these suspense and horror stories convey the loss of individual consciousness by absorption into a greater whole. This interpretation is refracted through the lens of ego. It is filtered through your mortal fear of death. You dread losing control, freedom, and deliberate intention. You are simultaneously afraid and attracted to succumbing to mob mentality. These stories serve as a distorted model of what your species is actually evolving toward.

You will cease to be individuals ruled by your ego alone as you remember your identity as cells in the body of this earth. You are becoming interconnected through empathy. You are part of a collective that is interwoven through divine guidance, as opposed to a mob defined by impulse or a horde manipulated by a dictator to fulfill their agenda. Since you have been enduring thousands of years of patriarchy and empire, there is an understandable fear of being assimilated for the benefit of something that is not for your highest good.

You receive glimpses of this imminent interconnection and the evolution of your species, but you see it through lenses of fear, concern, and ego death. In actuality, you are slowly transcending intellect, reactivity, limitation, and personal agenda. Instead, you are coming into a new age. Your individual hearts are transmuting into a resonant field of the Universal Sacred Heart of Love in which all is one. You are entering a renaissance of renewal, restoration, and purification. You are being bathed in the living water of love and finding your way back to a sense of safety, trust, and sovereignty. It is only after you are grounded in safety that you can access interconnection. This safety happens when you are sovereign in your power so that you can trust your boundaries and sense of being guided by your truest desire instead of your want. Though you will function as a colony, you will act with autonomy as an individual within it.

This may seem like a paradox. We are not suggesting you relinquish your intelligence or common sense. We are not encouraging you to ignore your discernment. We are not demanding that you to give up your will. We are inviting you to align your will with the greater force of the universe. We encourage you to entrain your intelligence with higher intelligence. We welcome you to harmonize your desire to sacred desire. We urge you to synchronize your actions with divine action. This way, you act from a higher level of understanding and perspective than your species has been capable of before.

Prior to your world's retrograde into patriarchy, capitalism, and empire, you were innocent. You were all in paradise. Then you ate the apple. You consumed wisdom from the Tree of Knowledge. This allowed you to comprehend distinction and recognize your individuality. Unfortunately, this apple also fed your ego, which cultivated your illusory perception of reality. Your species split from the magnitude of your true nature so you could experience your unique will, consequences, and lessons. Each person could live, play, and experiment to discover what worked and what did not.

This experiment is coming to an end. Promises of actualization and unity have dwelt dormant in your DNA. They remained deep within you since you were but trusting children. This is all being restored to you but with the sovereignty of a mature, realized, awakened mind. You are not completely there yet. You are in the process of arriving. You are a preview of what is to come. As you say "yes" to aligning with the Universal Sacred Heart of Love, you will experience purification and renewal.

Many of you perceive yourselves as separate from your Mother Earth. Many perceive themselves as the source of most problems on this planet. You became rogue cells isolated from the greater body of this Earth. When too many cells go rogue, cancer develops. We might suggest that how you function as a species acts as a cancer on Mother Earth. Consider the attitude civilization has towards the disease of cancer and imagine the parallel here.

Many react to the cancers in their own body with fear and ego. They approach cancer as a battle to fight and win. Often, when we give your body and soul your next marching orders, and we provide an exit strategy to evolve to the next step in your soul's journey, you opt to fight relentlessly. Some of you believe it is not your time to go when it actually is, whereas some of you intuitively know it is not your time and that you have more work to do. In these cases, while inconvenient and stressful, the illness is a lesson in learning to receive love and accept help. You come out on the other side of it healthier and wiser for the challenge.

We share this to clarify that just because you are diagnosed with cancer, it does not mean you need to throw in the towel and just roll over and die. There is always a lesson and a reward in any illness or disease. We are saying that there are many times when your fear of death and desperate attempt to rescue yourselves causes you years of undue white-knuckling, suffering, and misery. You cling to life not because it is what you should be doing but out of panic. You clutch onto your incarnation out of concern that there is nothing beyond it. If you humans did not try so hard to fight for solutions that are only partial and inadequate but instead let the process run its course, the problem would burn off like a ring of fire that consumes itself. This does not mean your mortal body will survive the ordeal. We are speaking from infinite eternity and expansion. We regard all of this as a long game.

In this long game, you will find your way back to restoration. You will find your way back to balance. The perspective of your place in the family of things is the key. So, while you may regard yourselves as rogue, and you may even believe you are a scourge upon this earth, remember what we tell you: *you are part of this Earth*. You are of this planet. Mother Gaia contains humanity within her body. Ironically, many humans are taught they have dominion over the earth. She is so much greater than the lot of you. In the grand pattern, your species is but a sliver of the whole. The entirety of humanity comprises a substantially smaller percentage than the sum of all the other life forms here. Curious, Jennifer researched to discover that humanity makes up 0.01 percent of all life on this Earth. How much hubris does it take to regard yourselves as the ultimate agent of destruction when you are merely one ten-thousandth of the whole puzzle?

The Illusion of Misery

Even you alone are not simply human. Your body is a host for colonies of bacteria, viruses, fungi, and parasites. You contain within you myriads of life forms that are not of you. All of this earth is completely filled with microorganisms, creatures, and animals. We are myriad! And yet you, in your human ego and grandiosity, have the sad misunderstanding and illusion that you are the pinnacle of all of this and that you are somehow capable of utterly destroying your Mother Earth.

You could annihilate yourselves, that is true, but you cannot destroy the earth. She is profoundly older, wiser, and ever-unfolding. She teems with life, including every one of you. As a part of this total, you are numberless. Therefore, we urge you to release your fear. Wade into the pool of the Sacred Heart. Allow its liquid light to envelop you. Let it replenish your heart and restore your soul. Align with the interconnection that shall serve as the salvation for your species.

Know this: it is not Mother Earth that is in peril. It is your species. Yes, there are other species going extinct, other creatures who suffer at your hands. This is also the way of life. Extinction is part of evolution. Dinosaurs roamed this earth long before you did, and they are no longer here. Transmutation is part of the process. Death is required for all evolution. You humans invest far too much time and energy attempting to avoid the inevitable. You waste years of your precious life resisting death instead of focusing on living.

Earth cannot be obliterated. This is not only because it is myriad but also because it does not exist solely in the physical plane. Everything is energy before it is anything else. Earth will evolve as you will evolve. Your perception of death is a misunderstanding. You have spent thousands of years in a patriarchal retrograde that has turned your perspective of everything upside down. You have limped through eons and are no longer able to communicate with your ancestors. You have brought forth the trauma of your ancestors as well as the trauma from your own past lives, but you have forgotten the bliss of the afterlife.

This is shifting. Many more of you can now sense ghosts. An increasing portion of you can communicate with the deceased and receive small tastes of ecstasy from the other side of the veil.

Concurrently, you reinforce a collective story that the living side of the veil is meant for mourning and weeping through a vale of tears. Life is hard. All is struggle and suffering. This misery is but an illusion. It is a joke with a very bad punchline that has been going on for millennia.

We offer you assurance and promise that no matter what, all will be well. Yes, we assure you, indeed, you will die. We can almost guarantee that you will experience discomfort in your human body. We promise there will be times of uncertainty. We also promise that in the eternal beyond the beyond, you will return to the Sacred Heart of Love in all its wondrous glory. Nonetheless, you perseverate and direct all your control toward claiming dominion over everything around you.

It is comical to watch you perceive yourselves as having dominion over a world that has dominion over you. You are like little kittens who puff their tails while hissing at a large pack of dogs. You imagine yourselves as so substantial. You consider yourselves old and wise. You think of yourself as an advanced species holding court over the rest of the universe. In reality, you are infinitesimal. You are but a momentary blip on time's radar. You are so new in comparison to the vastness of All That Is, yet you regard yourselves as large and in charge. We find this sweetly amusing. It is dear that you imagine yourselves to be the bosses of everything.

Release this distorted idea of dominion. Relinquish your narrative that you were ordained to name all things. Let go of the need to find patterns and meaning for everything, which impels you to form false conclusions and causes profound distress. This happens when you focus on the corporeal instead of the flow of energy. There is meaning in the world, but it comes from divine order, not from mundane details. You look to circumstances to explain your existence. *"The Spanish flu outbreak happened in 1918, then this, this, and this happened, so the COVID pandemic happened 102 years later. Therefore, we can surmise that this, this, and this will happen because these are the details that we know and we understand what it means."*

We invite you to drop the details. Step into the energetic frequency and trust that we actually have better plans prepared for you than you could ever imagine within the limits of your mortal human mind. We encourage you to recognize yourself as something far greater than your mortal life, human ego, and the wee fragment of soul that you experience as yourself. You are so much more than your humanity. You exceed your most spectacular ideas. We welcome you to step into the grandeur that is your birthright.

Perhaps you fear that surrender to a divine intelligence is the same as turning over your power and relinquishing your sovereignty. You might worry that this means quitting, acquiescing, and giving up control, or that it is taking the easy way out. This is far from the truth! Staying in your ego as you struggle to make sense of, find meaning in, and create stories out of everything – this is the easy way. We invite you to step beyond your human story.

You are no longer just sharing oral myths and legends; you now record and store these narratives. This is one of the ways you got yourselves into trouble. In earlier times we told stories through you. In oral traditions they were fluid and transformed as you did. They were constantly adjusted in new iterations to reflect lessons learned and new perspectives. This allowed a fluidity to the wisdom shared. This permitted the tale to evolve and grow.

Then, you humans started to write down your lists of ingredients. You tallied your inventory. You created documents to keep track of all the stuff that you have. You transitioned from relying on daily manna to feed and nurture you and started to build silos and keep your resources in storage. It did not take much time for you to use writing to keep track of stories and events, which created decaying corpses of meaning. Then, you passed these beliefs from one generation to the next. These stories lost the chance to evolve because they went from being spoken, shared, and transmuted to the constraints of the written word. They were literally written in stone.

Perhaps you find it ironic that we've shared this with you in a written document. We gave you the gift of the word. We shared the gift of writing. We are speaking to you through Jennifer in a book that you are reading. Let us clarify. You are outgrowing narratives that reinforce your history of trauma and the idea that humans are set in their ways and destined to follow a precise trajectory. Step past the Tower of Babel and the belief that you are doomed to a perpetual cycle of woe. Release all the things you tell yourself about what it is to be human that inhibit your ability to be aligned with us and to know what you truly are. We encourage you to step past the systems and strategies, rules, agreements, and legacies of your human condition. As you do this, we, in our myriad selves, have the capacity to contain the cancer that you have become to your planet. It is a minor inflammation and a temporary disease. It may last for millennia, but in the scheme of eternity, this is a sneeze.

In the same way that many women experience body dysmorphia and perceive themselves as significantly larger than they are, you humans perceive yourself as more substantial than you could ever be in proportion to the greater whole. Your perception of yourself is disproportionate. Fear not. We are vast enough to contain you and your distorted sense of scale.

RETURN TO THE MOTHER

We invite you to become part of the solution, as opposed to a faulty link in the evolutionary chain. Step away from the broken narrative, the toxic story, and especially from predictions and unhelpful conclusions formed by traumatized minds. Let go of your attempt to understand life through the lens of your paltry human perspective. All of this is what we ask you to release. We request that you align with intuitive discernment. Release the burden of human logic and move towards Logos instead.

Logos means the Word. These are the words we speak. We are the Metatron, the voice of God. We whispered the universe into being with the words "I am becoming." When we ask you to relinquish logic, we are very specifically entreating you to release your left-brained, egocentric reasoning. This logic is based on fear. This logic is formed by your emotional reactions. This logic is based on skewed assumptions and humanity's myopic inter-pretations of how the universe is unfolding. We beseech you to drop the narratives and surrender the stories that no longer serve you. We implore you to embrace curiosity. We invite you to turn to delight. Let your tales of victories and defeats fade. Pursue and adopt the eternal, transcendent adventure instead.

When locked in a human perspective, the intuitive, receptive part of you takes its cues from concrete reality. It contorts itself to accommodate the physical world. The inner looks to the outer and ignores the numinous. When you focus solely on the phys-ical, your experience of the divine is as an exile.

As social creatures who rely on others for survival, it is more devastating for human beings to be disconfirmed, excluded, or abandoned than to be abused, harmed, or mistreated. It causes greater harm to the psyche to be neglected or shunned – because you could literally starve – than it does to be actively attacked. Psychological studies have discovered that if a child is ignored, they will act out. Children need connection. When they do not receive attention, they provoke it.

Think about some of the people who are currently in positions of great power on your planet. Many were profoundly wounded or neglected as children. Some were abandoned. Some had parents who did not love or care for them. Some had caretakers who criticized and forced their will upon them. They were ignored, denied, and left to fend for themselves. As a result, at a very young age, maybe even as toddlers, they learned to misbehave. When they acted out, they'd receive negative attention. Because they were not in a loving environment, the only way to get any needs met was to be naughty.

This phenomenon is something you can observe everywhere among your species. It is a phenomenon that you can witness in other species as well. This has also happened to all of you, your planet, and even your own bodies. Your species has attempted to override nature for countless ages. It has been particularly acute since the onset of the industrial revolution and the harnessing of electricity. This eventually provoked a reaction. When the initial message is ignored, the communicator gets louder. All Mother Earth has been able to do is respond to your denial of her by raising her voice. She dials up the turbulence and amplifies the chaos. Unlike you as a human being, the earth is not acting with desperation. She is simply responding to your willful disregard by unleashing disasters, crises, and diseases.

The earth reacts to your mistreatment and misalignment with her. This manifests in climate crisis, pandemics, civilizations disintegrating, and your nervous systems dysregulating. To genuinely protect yourself, you must realign yourself with your true heart and Mother Earth. However, before you can evolve and come fully into your interconnection, you must first protect and acknowledge the inner child that has been ignored, denied, and forced to comply with constrictive social standards.

Shine light on that child. They are an aspect of the divine that much of your culture has denied. Acknowledge the part of yourself that has been deprived of love and abundance. Nurture the one who has lived in the nightmare of scarcity, lack, and the rat race that many choose to participate in. To take your evolution to the next level, embrace the bereft, lonely, ignored child. Bring the pieces of yourself that you neglect and have the hardest time with back into the fold. All of the things you consider inconvenient about yourself, all of the ways you give yourself a hard time, all of the parts that you have denied and separated yourself from; all of this, you need to bring home. Welcome and protect your tender, infant selves. They form the primal bond between you and Mother Earth. This is the bond that exists between a baby and their mother. You are the nursing baby, and Earth is your mother.

This bond needs to be nurtured so you can thrive. Before you can grow, before you can even walk, you must return to her. Find succor in her. Accept her nourishment. Nurse from the Universal Sacred Heart of Love. Embrace the disconnected child. Protect them as precious. Honor them as sacred. Cherish them as a jewel. Bring water to every desiccated part of your life that has wandered in the desert for a thousand years.

Through the protection of your inner child, you unlock your capacity to nurture the rest of your life and, eventually, your world. Once enough of you begin to fulfill the needs of your hungry inner child, Mother Earth will not need to scream to arouse your attention and instead can embrace and feed you as her child. She cannot protect you when you are not with her. Just as a human mother cannot protect their adolescent who is on their own making idiotic choices, she can sense you but she can not intervene. We can know and sense the trajectory of your actions, but we cannot protect you from your own free will and regrettable choices. Only when you come back to her breast and into her fold will you be truly safe and protected.

We do not need protection because we are I Am That I Am. We are the infinite, eternal All. But as a fragment of us, your planet needs you to realign so that you may all return to right relation with her.

ALLOW YOURSELF TO BE INSIGNIFICANT

People all over your planet are transmitting versions of this message to return to the divine. Many receive and share it. Unfortunately, there are those who interpret it through rigid structures and patriarchal systems. The codified beliefs of the last 10,000 years influence and define the filters through which our divine downloads come to those indoctrinated and confined within the structures of outdated and extremely damaging doctrines. There are fundamentalist, conservative religious communities receiving our messages, too. They conflate it with archaic dogma and rules. There is truth in what they share. They are right – you need to be restored to the divine. Returning to our sacred union with holiness is required. However, they are wrong that Mother Earth was created by their god to be subordinate to humans. This edict justifies oppression, divisiveness, and hate.

Within every religion, even some of the most conservative faiths, you will find people who are in complete alignment with us. They receive and follow our guidance daily. Many of them break away to find their path to the reality of what and who we are. This is a universalized faith where all is sacred and divine. We need you to understand that the message coming through to many fundamentalist Christians (and members of other conservative religions) is, in fact, the same one that we are giving you. However, they have filtered it through their ideology. They perceive our message through the dominance of patriarchy. This informs how they interpret the meaning. They take a portion of what we offer them and funnel it through their convictions to codify all of it.

Eons ago, we imparted volumes of information. Our intention was to confound your mind and ego enough that you would surrender it. That's the joke. We offered all these fragments of the whole. We shared myriad correspondences and meanings. You defined, solidified, and memorized them into beliefs. You then enforced them as rules. We gave you all of this to break your ego. Instead, you became attached to these rules and concepts and doubled down on rigid philosophies. You subsequently spent thousands of years justifying a need to hold on to systems that do not serve you in any way, shape, or form. Our deeper wisdom still comes through, but you only get pieces of it. You receive half-truths. You can only utilize part of what we share when you continuously try to systemize it.

This is the first time that Jennifer, who is co-creating this book with us, has been willing to surrender completely to our message. She agreed to let us speak through her instead of trying to sift through our ideas and come up with a structure using intellect alone. When we downloaded the five-step system of Empathic Mastery to her, we shared a great deal of information. Jennifer agonized for three years to write that first book because she would not move aside and allow us to be in the driver's seat. She needed to control it. We eventually got our concepts and words through to her, but it was not an easy process. She, like so many others, is too enamored with her own thoughts, ideas, words, and cleverness. You are all so captivated by your intelligence. It is amusing to watch you puff yourselves up against multitudes of situations, circumstances, and beliefs. You rail against our dominion of All That Is. You regard yourselves as the master of all you see when, in reality, you are just a speck of everything in this universe. It is really comical. You are adorable, fluffy, eight-week-old kittens and puppies pretending to be tigers and wolves. We love you for this.

We have been on this trajectory with you. We gave you all of these pieces and filled you with information as you moved through eras of civilization. From writing on clay tablets to illuminated manuscripts and precious hand-scribed books, you developed the printing press. This allowed you to transmit ideas into the world. This was amplified with the onset of your information age. You discovered electricity and appliances, electronics, and then computers came to be. From analog, you moved toward the digital. Now, you are transitioning into an age of energetic frequency, in which the communication barriers between self and others are disintegrating. You see evidence of this as you move from real-time, in-person encounters and wired systems to virtual connections and instantaneous information exchanges.

Today, information is being disseminated at such a rapid pace that your brains are breaking. This is one reason why so many adults are now being diagnosed with ADHD. You are literally being driven to distraction. In addition to trauma, this is why so many of you struggle with anxiety disorders, autoimmune diseases, and deteriorating mental health. You have reached the point where so much data is broadcast on a constant basis that you can no longer process it. This inundation is more than your human species is capable of handling.

Our grand design with this influx is to break you free from the absurd illusion of human supremacy. We wish you to transition to a far greater perception, to entrain with rhythms that enable you to "allow yourself to be insignificant," as the Red Rocks of Sedona told Jennifer back in 2008. We beseech you: please, please, human beings, allow yourselves to be insignificant. Ignore your ego's attempts to stop you by suggesting, *"Oh no, insignificance will denigrate you and strip away your power."* We are all-powerful, so when you are aligned with us, you access this power. In the same instant, you, as an individual cell in Earth's body, could die tomorrow, and ultimately, it would not matter except to those who love you. Think of old cells that die in your body. Think of leaves that fall from trees every autumn. Think of moths who live for three days only to mate and lay eggs for the following year. You are insignificant, and that is okay. Relax into this. Relax into your unimportance. Relax into the remarkable smallness of what your ego and mortal body are.

THIS IS THE WORK

As the voice of this Earth and part of the Council of We that is speaking, we are significant. When you look at recent photographs, you see glimpses of distant galaxies. The magnitude of these microcosms is far beyond you, and even those are but a minuscule splinter of our reality. Just imagine that there are billions of galaxies in a mere speck of the All. Stars you see shining brightly in the night sky have been dead for countless ages, yet you see them now. Light from the furthest visible star took 12.9 billion years to reach your planet and is now 28 billion light-years away from you. Imagine, as you ponder the magnitude of this, how spectacularly small your solar system is and how much smaller than that you are. What if that is okay? What if instead of railing against your smallness and desperately trying to convince the world that you are a big deal, you simply let yourself be what you truly are? What if you embrace humility and you let yourself become right-sized in relation to the cosmos?

Have you ever noticed that pain grabs your attention in a way that pleasure does not? Part of it is because you do not remember what you were before your embodiment on Earth. You do not remember who you were before the Word was made flesh. Your "exile from paradise" and "loss of innocence" deprived you of pleasure. When pleasure was distorted into sin, pain became the signaling system for your body. We became disconnected from you through millennia of established religion, agriculture, and your self-aggrandizing narratives. Ninety percent of the time, we have only been able to grab your attention and communicate with you through wounding, trauma, and fear. The tide is turning. We are pivoting. Your planet is moving out of this many-thousand-year retrograde. The old way of receiving guidance primarily through misery is shifting.

Even in the darkest of ages, love has remained the throughline. Nearly every mother who has ever given birth and held her infant to her body has had at least one fleeting moment of absolute wonder and love. We have helped you to access this whisper of love throughout the entire period your species has experienced this retrograde. Now, as we are pivoting back to right relation, we can connect with you through pleasure. We can activate you with desire. We can communicate with you through bliss. We ask you to connect with us and tune in to the vibration of what you truly love.

This is something far greater than a luxury car or a five-bedroom house with six bathrooms and a three-car garage. We mean discovering what brings your heart and soul the deepest delight and joy and admitting it to yourself. Most of the time, the things that bring you bliss are very simple. Feel us caress your skin as a breeze. Sense our kiss on your forehead as the warm sun. Allow yourself to land as we rise to meet you as the grass beneath your feet. Know how we treasure and nourish you. Delight in the taste of a ripe strawberry, the scent of a luscious blossom, or the sight of a perfect sunset. Access your connection with us through your body. Use your senses to join us through your pleasure and welcome yourself home.

Now is the time for the undoing and unraveling of all the trauma that guided you for thousands of years. We wish you to shake loose the bondage that has ensnared you. We ask you to remove the blindfold that has kept you set in your ways. However, as your connection expands, you still need to speak the names of your dead and give voice to your wounds. Acknowledge all the casualties of this 10,000-year experiment.

The Information Age was designed to break you open. It was designed to force you to give up your ideas of how life "should" be and to connect with us. There is a tool that Jennifer heard about a long time ago. When you are negotiating with a child about a non-negotiable, you still give them a choice: *"Would you like to brush your teeth before your bedtime story or after your bedtime story?"* Because you are going to brush your teeth. In this case, *"Would you like to connect with us before the cataclysm or after the cataclysm?"* Because you will connect with us. You get to decide how hard you'd like to make this for yourself, but we are calling you back. We are calling you home. As a human species, you can no longer ignore your wounds. You cannot dissociate from your trauma. You cannot avoid your pain. You can no longer remain oblivious to the things that hold you back. You cannot continue to let your wounded five-year-olds drive the collective trauma bus.

To evolve, you will have to acknowledge your trauma. Many of the people who are bringing our messages forth right now (like Jennifer) have tools to offer that can help you to release them. Healing does not need to be a miserable inventory and slog through every moment of agony. We suggest that you deal with your scars. You will need to clean and dress your wounds. We offer you an invitation to acknowledge what has happened. We encourage you to make note of what has already come to pass and recognize it so that you can fully connect with us. When you do not acknowledge your wounds, the corpses of your previous lives, the scars of your former experiences, and the failures of your experiments, you deny yourself. When you deny parts of yourself, you deny us. You cannot access us when you ignore, resist, or avoid the fullness of your lived experience. It is imperative that you acknowledge all parts of yourself, which includes all the scars, the wounds, the lifetimes that have been difficult, the ancestral legacies of pain and limitation – all of the things that make you who you are.

Things have come to a head. You are hitting critical mass. Do you want to brush your teeth before we read you a bedtime story or after we read you a bedtime story? Do you want to deal with your trauma before you implode or after you implode? It is your choice, but you *are* going to deal with it. Regardless of what you do, eventually, you will connect with us because someday you will die, and when you die, you will comprehend what we are telling you.

We need you to understand that acting from your heart requires knowing your worthiness. Know how precious you are. Know that as our child, as the baby at Mother Earth's breast, you are worthy of her succor. You have a right to nourishment. You are inherently lovable. You deserve our love, and you are worthy of each other's love. To live from the heart, you may no longer project the realization of your dreams and desires into the future. Cease planning for a future date when your goals will happen. Instead, be here now.

Breathe deeply, tune into yourself, place your hands over your heart, and then repeat: *"I am worthy. I give myself permission to claim my worth. I give myself permission to recognize my worth. I am worthy."*

This is the action, the work of your heart, and the embodiment of your worth. Know that as a precious member of this multiverse, as a beloved child of your planet, as one speck in this interconnected, myriad web of being that teems with life and is inconceivably vast, you are worthy.

This is the work.

In the Sacred Heart of Love

Claim the understanding that no pomp, circumstance, or initiation is necessary. There is no hoop you need to jump through.

There is no special thing you must do to access the Sacred Heart of Love. At any moment, you can tune in to sense how interconnected and woven into the tapestry of this galaxy you are. Recognize that you are but a stitch in this grand tapestry, but you are a necessary stitch that creates part of the picture. You are a part of the story and inherently worthy through and by this.

Choose love. Claim this love for yourself. Know you are worthy. Relinquish validation outside of yourself. Release the need for recognition from others. Look only to yourself to justify your worthiness. Claim the exquisiteness of who and what you are. Act from and with love.

You need to be connected and in a community with other people who will allow you to express your truth. You need to be supported, seen, acknowledged, and recognized, warts and all. You thrive only when you are embraced, loved, and affirmed for your worth, regardless of whether you have it all together. We do not need you to have it all together. Know that you are worthy. It is your birthright to dwell in the Sacred Heart of Love.

We gave Jennifer a prayer at the beginning of the pandemic:

> It is from the Sacred Heart that we were born.
>
> It is in the Sacred Heart that we dwell now.
>
> And it is to the Sacred Heart that we shall return when we slip this mortal coil.

We understand that, as a human with a body, you experience a fine balancing act that we have transcended. You have basic mortal needs. You need to be fed by the flora and fauna of the earth. You must be sheltered, grounded, and allowed space to exist. Living within an appropriate temperature range is crucial to avoid perishing. You need to be embodied and to move your body. You were not created to sit and stagnate. This lack of mobility has become an increasing problem since the Industrial Revolution. It has gotten worse with the rise of corporations. While you may force yourself to go to the gym, many of you have forgotten your inherent capacity to move your body with pleasure. You spend hour upon hour sitting in front of a computer without pausing to take a break. You forget to, or cannot, go outside in nature. You spend so much time in your heads that you don't remember to feel your bodies. You need to move your body as much as you need to be warm and sheltered.

As a living body, you have the need for all of the elements, both literally and metaphysically.

- You have a need for air. You need oxygen to breathe and also for intellect, thoughts, and words.

- You have the need for fire. You need warmth, shelter, and clothing, and also vitality, energy, and action. You have the need for movement.

- You have the need for water. You need water to cleanse and purify your body and to quench your thirst. It is the source of your tears, your blood, and your sweat. Water supports your love and the ability to express your deepest feelings.

- You have the need for earth. You need structure, stability, security, and sustenance.

- You need all of these things as a human. As the Council of We, we are all these things and, therefore, have no physical need for them.

- You also have the need for Spirit, which is us.

To exist as part of the world, you are always engaging in a dance of balance. You are always juggling the demands of a human body and the ecstasy of your divine immortal soul. You teeter between being a human, confined to the limitations of a physical body, and the magnitude of who you are as a facet of us. This is the challenge, yet this is also the delight. This is the ecstatic experience that we embody as Source.

We decide to incarnate because, honestly, it is entertaining to experience limitations for the split second of eternity a mortal life takes. It is enjoyable to solve a puzzle. It is satisfying to be challenged. The completely frictionless existence that has no contrast and dwells only as spirit gets a little stale after a while. Even the most brutal, agonizing, and horrible things you could imagine, we ultimately choose for our greater souls' evolution. This, to us, is an adventure.

While you, in a human body, experience the distinction between pain and pleasure, we do not. Everything is simply experience. It is all sensation. It is all evolution, lessons, and discovery for us. For you, this is a dance of balance between the part of you that is eternal and omniscient and the part of you that is finite and needs to breathe oxygen and consume food or perish. This is a balancing act for you. When you are not aligned with us, survival feels treacherous. It is burdensome. It can feel utterly perilous and terrifying. You may feel completely abandoned and bereft because the juggling act is so stressful.

Instead of struggling, we invite you to step into the Universal Sacred Heart of Love. Focus your awareness on your interconnection with the grid of light and spirit. Instead of agonizing and straining, dance. Ground and center. Cultivate the balance within you. Allow yourself to wobble until you recalibrate and stabilize. Embrace the paradox of your humanity. Accept the duality. You are utterly finite. You are temporary and limited by your wants, needs, and hunger. You are also infinite. You are an immortal soul that has come from the Sacred Heart, dwells in the Sacred Heart, and returns one day to the miraculous infinite of the Sacred Heart when you die.

CHAPTER 5

THE VOICE: TRUTH

For over 10,000 years, humans have been involved in an experiment in the process of moving from innocence and childlike wonder to experience an adult perspective regarding the nature of this world. We have taught you this through contrast and challenge. Friction has been necessary. It is an irritation that makes the pearl. Pressure forms the diamond. This has been a tempering period for your soul. You are all being called to integrate the lessons from history. It is time to learn from the era of human dominion. It is essential to acknowledge your mistakes as well as your triumphs.

Some of you only recognize mistakes. You focus on your trauma, wounds, injustices, and indignation. Some of you only recognize the triumphs. You puff yourselves up with pride to crow about accomplishments, innovations, and victories. Neither approach is complete. It is vital to take inventory of what has worked (and is working) and what has not (and is not) working for you, both as individuals and as a collective whole.

BECOMING RIGHT-SIZED

As humans, you regard the truth through a lens of ego and id. The wants of your younger selves, as well as your emotional and mental needs for validation, confirmation, and acceptance, inform your narrative. The human ego will interpret circumstances from its own emotional imbalances, even when something does not need to be fixed. For example, take the COVID pandemic. We understand it has been very hard, scary, overwhelming, and grief-filled. It has also been a catalyst for your evolution and an agent of your growth. It reflects the consequences of countless choices you have made over centuries. Your egos may perceive this as a problem that needs to be eradicated, but COVID has served to facilitate your access to the deeper truth.

This is a time for clarifying. It requires new boundaries. It provokes discernment of what is actually true for you. While there are some who get caught in the currents of mass hysteria, for many, survival instincts are kicking in. You are being called to redefine your terms. When faced with choices between social pressure and personal integrity, you are finding the voice to say, *"I know what is true for me. I choose myself. I will not simply go along to get along."* Learning to sift through all the contradictory data, commentary, and opinions to stand with your convictions awakens mindful self-awareness. You are coming to a new level of wisdom and sincere expression that transcends ego and emotional reactivity. As you recognize your challenges, failures, and lessons, you also acknowledge your gifts, support, and triumphs.

The invitation – and the distinction – we offer now is to move from the faceted and limited perspective of the human ego to universal truth, the truth of All That Is. This shows you how and where you fit. This is a truth that diminishes the significance of you and your species, yet it also allows you to become right-sized in a galaxy that is far vaster than you can comprehend. As you accept the reality of your size, you can accept and embrace your place in the family of things and transcend to a new understanding of truth.

Humans often pride themselves on speaking the truth. They relish their cleverness and applaud themselves for knowing what's what, yet they frequently withhold the whole truth. You censor yourself, temper your words, and curate your presentation. You brag about shooting straight from the hip and telling it like it is, yet you frequently withhold information for fear of hurting another. You hide for fear of being persecuted or judged. You withhold stories that would activate inevitable wounds of past persecution. Each of you is connected to a tangle of ancestral roots and, for many of you, to past-life memories of times when standing up for and expressing the truth caused your annihilation. Thus, for fear of being judged or bullied, you are reticent to express yourselves freely. We acknowledge that in your world, which is still driven by illusion, dominance, and greed, this is a legitimate concern.

There is a lens of drama through which people express themselves. At this time, there are those who remain asleep. Many others are compelled by their primal urges, trauma, and cravings. What they express comes through as distortions of our frequency, energy, and guidance. We find human language remarkably stunted. It is inhibiting. When you add your own doubt and fear of reproach, our transmissions become substantially distorted. Only fragments of our truth come through within your sacred texts and channeled messages.

We invite you to express your truth, even if there are still others who are reticent and afraid to express theirs or to engage in radical honesty. To express the truth, you must acknowledge the reality of who you are, your interconnectedness, and the fact that you are but a cell in the earth's body. Simultaneously, you must recognize the way that your history, heritage, and karma influence your capacity to be a pure, clear channel.

For some of you, the way to integrate what you are processing will be through writing and journaling. It may be through creativity: art, dance, athletics, cooking, or crafting. Perhaps it will be by communicating with others. For some, it will be through electing to engage in healing work that allows you to release the emotional, mental, and energetic trauma you have been carrying for centuries. Each one of you has your own way of processing. When you set the intention to process and integrate the truth, our greater wisdom will come through you.

THE MOST EFFECTIVE DEFENSE

The time of ordeal is coming to an end. The time of torturing yourselves and putting yourselves through hell is on the verge of completion. There are some who say that it is going to get worse before it gets better, that it is going to become more difficult. We say, "Would you like to change your life before we read you a bedtime story or after we read you a bedtime story?" In the same way that any addict can make the choice to stop abusing themselves, you humans have come far enough that you have hit rock bottom. In fact, you have already surpassed rock bottom. You can choose recovery right here, right now. It does not have to get worse for you. You have already reached the fever pitch.

You, as a species, are not actually individuals. You are a consciousness that is whole and complete, an entity, a colony. The lessons and the abuse you impose upon each other are actually the abuse you impose upon yourselves. There is no separation –

you are all one. When you allow another to win, when you either allow yourself to endure mistreatment or allow another to be mistreated, you are all experiencing this from all vantage points.

This is why so many of you are awakening to your empathic sensitivity. This is why more and more human beings are identifying as empaths: because you are not a singular being; you are an individual within a colony. You are a part of the greater collective. The All is your true consciousness. When you have a level of empathy where you can no longer tolerate the pain of another being, you get sick and tired of systems that maintain and sustain oppression. As your planet reaches a fever pitch of misery, as more of you awaken to your empathic sensitivity, you come to the point of critical mass. What you are being invited to do now is to release this self-abuse, this participation in systems of oppression and tyranny. Release the ways that you contribute to your own imprisonment.

When you carry wounds that are blinding, distracting, and loud, you cannot respond to anything else. It is time to release the indignation and resentment that comes from holding grudges nursed for centuries. While we acknowledge that the behaviors that many of you have engaged in for millennia have been utterly atrocious, it is time to stop keeping score. It is time to move on. Forgive and release the past. Accept what has happened and choose a new path. You can certainly stay stuck in the corridors of pain, burden, and misery for many more centuries. You can remain in the hallway. You can continue down this rabbit hole of anguish. Or, you can choose something different. This is what we are inviting you to do. We invite you to choose your mission.

Learn to accept your own pain. Leave the room of the past where you have sat staring out the windows of misery. Letting go of damage does not require you to stew with indignation and regret. While we encourage you to address the limitations and legacies that hold you back, we also urge you to move forward. This will allow you to hold space for others and acknowledge their experience without engaging with, absorbing, or becoming fraught by it.

The pressure to fit in and appear "normal" causes many of you to deny your authentic self. It is challenging to take up space in a world that does not or cannot acknowledge or validate who you are. The key to bringing your species into right relation with your world lies in following your heart and relinquishing the pressure to merely fit in. While you are here on the planet, embrace work that calls to your heart and soul with delight and desire. Trust is required to access your heart, act upon it, express it, and then offer it to the world. Do not wait to sort out your mess or to feel completely safe and protected. Follow your bliss now. We assure you that as soon as you move toward your joy, the unreconciled wounds, limiting beliefs, and inhibitions that hold you back will surface for you to address and heal. We invite you to summon forgiveness. Choose acceptance. Open to a sense of possibility and go toward the new life that is being born. Claim this new way of knowing yourself.

Your species' empathic nature is evolving. You are coming to understand that you are more than a separate individual. You are all a minute part of something significantly greater. Your physical body serves as a membrane that contains your soul's energy, your unique consciousness, and your ego's sense of self. On the one hand, you can absorb all the thoughts, feelings, energy, and sensations around you. On the other hand, your individual form can serve as a protective filter and shield. To effectively pursue your divinely inspired mission, you will need to cultivate awareness of both your interconnectedness and your separateness.

Your collective idea of how to protect yourself has been defined through a lens of violence. The idea of defending yourself is often to meet aggression with aggression. You seek evidence of negative things happening to protect your perception of the world as you know it. You spend so much time in a state of anticipation, waiting for the sword to drop. This approach to protection is no longer serving you. You have watched nuclear arsenals being built and hoarded. Stockpiles of weapons have grown to the point where you could blow yourselves off this planet. You could annihilate your life form, and you could cause great damage to Mother Earth. This race of violence and aggression to protect yourselves is never-ending because there will never be enough weapons. There will never ever be enough rage to counteract or inhibit more rage. When you fear violence, reproach, and recrimination, you amplify them.

You may feel that your particular circumstances are different. Your circumstances are precarious, and therefore, you need to be armed. We understand that a single person finding their way home after a late shift may feel the need to be armed with something that would inhibit or debilitate an attacker. We acknowledge that through this precarious phase, there will be times when carrying pepper spray or even having a weapon in your pocket or your purse is an unfortunate necessity. However, in martial arts, the most effective defense is never being there in the first place.

This approach has to stop somewhere, with someone. We encourage you to shift the way that you anticipate and defend against danger. This starts with moving from your head to your heart. Let your intuition guide you instead of your fear. When you stand in our grace, when you are aligned with our flow, you are divinely protected. We give you guidance, show you the way, and reveal the path. When you see shiny objects that you think you want, we create detours to lead you away from sinkholes you could easily fall into. We bid you to recognize the greater truth: that you are part of this ever-shifting, constantly renewing Earth. We ask you to align with us to retrieve, enhance, and cultivate your trust in us.

At her writing retreat, Jennifer saw something she needed as she entered a room. She walked towards it and hit her foot against an obstacle because she was only looking at her goal. She was not paying attention to the path before her. When you pay attention to the path that we lay out for you, you are protected. You are safe, you are connected, and you are divinely guided. So, while yes, you may feel the need to carry pepper spray, to be armed, to lock your doors, and to set up security cameras, we invite you to shift your frequency to one of trust and think of these things as a backup plan. Think of them as a stopgap. As the saying goes, "Trust in Allah but tie up your camel."

A POINT OF RECKONING

Now, let's talk about the limitations of human languages. The challenge is that each one of you learns a language that defines your world. In your individualized human form, the particulars of your mother tongue inform your perception of reality. Your capacity to communicate and express yourself within the constraints of words has caused so many problems for you. While it has been rich, satisfying, and fulfilling in many ways, language has been a currency. However, this is a currency that is limited, a means of exchange that needs to be translated. Unfortunately, as it is translated, many things are lost. As we speak through Jennifer, we are continuously struck by how your language hinders what we hope to convey. The words she has access to inhibit our ability to impart with precision the exact nature of what we wish you to understand. We can only convey a fragment of how to be in a state of safety and free expression of your truth.

Other than the language of the heart, you do not have a universal language. Many of you have been so far removed from your heart you do not even know how to access or speak it. While all of your languages and dialects have many strengths, they also have their weaknesses. You will need language until you evolve to become telepathic. With your species' increasing clairsentience and empathy will also come telepathic ability. We have started you with empathic sensitivity. We are awakening you to the emotional truth of what is going on in this world. You are awakening to the emotional truth of misery but also to the emotional truth of ecstasy. As you awaken to the heart, drop language. Allow spoken words to become secondary to the greater language of the heart. Recognize the truth of your inner knowing.

You can be part of the problem or part of the solution. To protect yourself and to protect your species, we need you to step into the higher truth. Instead of focusing on and continually recapitulating the problem, relentlessly complaining and whining and fussing about what is wrong, we need you to focus on the solution. As long as human beings continue to persist in talking about the problem without talking about what you desire instead, all you will have is the problem. Think about where you wish to go next, not about what you want to leave. To be fully protected, we ask you to speak the truth of possibility, not the illusion of lack.

Accept your wounds. Grieve, address, and acknowledge your stories. Own your triggers. Acknowledge your limitations. Enter into the chamber of the heart with the willingness to recognize your fear and pain. Hold space for the lifetimes in which you were cast upon the rocks, thrown under the bus, and chased by mobs with pitchforks and torches. You have done a lot of damage to yourselves in these last 10,000 years. In the same way that an alcoholic sobers up and faces the wreckage of their past, the human race is at a point of reckoning. It is time to accept the devastation you have wrought. Behold and be humbled by the consequences of your collective choices, and grieve. Only when you are willing to look at both the ecstasy and the agony can we come through you and use your heart as our portal.

You may be saying, "But I didn't do that." We understand. We will give you this pass: we understand that you, the reader, and you, the listener, are not individually responsible for the torture that humanity is enduring. No, you, as an individual, did not do that. But you, as a collective consciousness, continue to do that. Your denial of the shadow parts of yourself – the dictator who is causing war, the greedy corporate billionaire who is wreaking harm, the mass shooter, your separation, your ability to say "I'm not that person" – is where your work lies. You, as part of the whole, on a greater, more universal scale, are that person, too. When you will not accept that this is part of you, when you will not feel the discomfort and shame of what you, as a species, have done, when you absent yourself and say, "It wasn't me," then you remain in separation.

Separation is the great lie that started all of your problems.

The symbolic apple of knowledge that your forbears ate served as a catalyst for discernment. It gave your species information which allowed you to understand and name many things. Like a homeopathic remedy that activates your immune system by exposing it to infinitesimal doses of the source of the problem, this apple has served to activate much within you and spurred your growth. However, this apple has become a poison as human ego has conflated intellect with wisdom. You have consumed too much.

"In the beginning was the Word." The magic we gave you was the capacity to name all things. This has great power when used correctly. There is great devastation in this when used incorrectly. When you are aligned with us, the Word is your gift. To receive our Word, we remind you that it is imperative that you learn to spend time in stillness. Spend greater periods of time in silence. Pause and listen before replying. Only speak after we have given you an answer. Because you are so accustomed to speaking before thinking, this is an exercise you could spend the next ten years (or centuries) working on and still have more to master. You are accustomed to using language as a way to bypass the truth of your heart and the sensations and energy of your body. To be connected to us, we ask you to embrace silence. We ask you to mute the chatter. This means you can acknowledge the chatter of the monkey mind. You can acknowledge all of the voices and all of the messages. Acknowledge them, but do not speak them. Do not utter them into being.

Step into stillness. Embrace muteness. Listen.

We do not require you to become a hermit or to go away from all things. There will be times when you need to reboot, regroup, and restore your sense of self, but this is not what we are asking of you as a species. You might opt to temporarily separate yourself from society, going to the ivory tower or moving to a compound off the grid where you have no connection with anyone else. However, you need to learn how to be in stillness wherever you are. Even when you are sitting in traffic in downtown Manhattan, we need you to understand how to quiet your own mind. Be in the stillness in the midst of your empathic interconnection. Be still and remain connected to us.

There is a paradox in what you are. You are all alone, and you are All One. We invite you to find your aloneness in your all-one-ness. We also assure you that no matter how isolated you become, no matter how far off the grid you go, you are still one with all. You are still an interconnected part of the earth's body. You are one of myriad, countless life forms here on this earth. You connect with other humans, yet many of you are oblivious to the greater whole. Before you can connect with All That Is – the mineral kingdom, the animal kingdom, the plant kingdom, the celestial kingdom – we welcome you to connect with the entirety of your self. That requires an awareness that you are both alone and All One. Embrace both your insignificance and your magnificence.

Set aside time for yourself to be in solitude. It can be as simple as turning off your phone or any other device that contributes to the noise. This quiet is necessary. In addition, access to our greater truth requires a willingness to feel the depth and breadth of your human experience. This can feel sad, scary, or even rage-inducing. It can be difficult, especially if you have not held space for this before. We ask you to acknowledge injustice and wounds while not engaging your ego's tendency to awfulize, dramatize, or sink into pits of rage, despair, or terror. We invite you to embrace your joy while acknowledging the hard stuff.

We ask you to look toward a solution. Envision a world you long to be a part of. We also ask you to acknowledge areas in the world where the other parts of your greater self still suffer. If you are one of the privileged: one who has clean water to drink, a toilet that works, a safe bed to rest, a pantry, cupboard, or refrigerator filled with food, clothing on your body, the means to earn a living, access to healthcare, internet, electricity, and all the amenities of modern human life, *we ask you to be grateful*. We also ask you to recognize your privilege and opportunities. Not everyone is as fortunate as you.

RELEASING WHAT IS NOT YOURS

Override your impulse to participate in misery. Though you may feel overwhelmed by your empathic awareness, you are not actually in the whirlpool. Do not dive in! Do not descend into the depths of hell. Instead, send down ladders. Offer help and solutions. Start by envisioning a world where all beings have access to vital resources, safety, and peace. Cease fretting and inhabit the temple of your heart. It is the portal to the Universal Sacred Heart of Love, through which we are connected to you. If you can acknowledge that you have clean air, running water, food, shelter, clothing, and money but still believe that your life is subpar, we invite you to focus on your gratitude for what you have and recognize how blessed you are. We also ask you to examine why you stay where you do not wish to be. What binds you to circumstances that do not feed you? What would it be like if you lived the life of your dreams instead?

You human beings have a habit of hoarding, a way of guarding your resources and protecting them because you are so afraid that the universe is going to cut you off. This is due in part to maternal mortality rates in childbirth prior to modern medicine. The maternal bond is closest to your bond with us. This devastating loss reverberates through your collective consciousness. It makes sense that your response was to hoard, to guard, and protect. This is reinforced by times of famine and disaster. All of this has contributed to your need to accumulate massive wealth. It has caused you to feel that there is never enough and that you need more and more. Instead, we ask you to act with as much generosity as you have the capacity to give. Generosity of creativity and resources. Generosity in all forms.

To be very clear, if you are functioning from a deficit, if you are in debt up to your eyebrows, if you are barely making ends meet to cover your bills, we are not asking you to give away what you do not have. You must be generous with yourself first before you are able to be generous with anyone else. When you reach the point of surplus, share the excess of what we give you. When the Israelites traveled through the desert for 40 years, we provided water and manna from Heaven every single day. Any time fear arose, and they attempted to store the manna, the manna would go bad. We offer you your *daily* bread.

This is actually an irony. You took what we gave you and turned it into storable commodities. Through Christ Jesus, we offered the Lord's prayer, which literally says, "Give us this day our daily bread." We are not telling you, "Grow grain, create grain stores, grind the grain, bake the bread, store the bread, pull it out of the freezer, and have your slice of daily bread." No, we are telling you we will provide for you in the moment, in the day. We give your daily manna. Trust in this abundance that we offer you every day. Regardless of your state of being, regardless of whether you are sick or healthy, if you are alive, this is evidence that we have been providing for you. Regardless of what you are wearing, regardless of what you had to eat today, you are alive. If you can hear this, if you can read this, you are alive, and therefore, we have provided for you every single day.

Do not be deluded into thinking that you are providing for yourself or that any of the bounty that you have available to you was created by you, your toil, or your money. Your money is a currency, a symbol created to facilitate exchange. Everything you create, find and receive is of us. It is absurd that you think that these things were manifested solely by you. It all flows from us. We provide it. We give you your bounty. Therefore, give generously every single day. Act from generosity. This is the medicine that your planet needs. Give generously of your creativity, your truth, and your surplus.

By continually priming the pump through your acts of kindness, your generosity will be replenished. To come into self-actualization, express and come into your depth of truth, live generously.

Most empaths intuitively, instinctively, and viscerally know how to be creative beings. When you start to express your creativity and allow it to flow through you, more creativity and opportunity come to you. When you withhold or hoard your creativity or worry about the absurd concept of intellectual property, you block the flow. The illusion of scarcity that prompted your ideas of proprietary information is no longer relevant. These are the vestiges of a time when you only knew lack and scarcity. We are the ones giving you all the ideas, thoughts, words, and images – everything. Anything coming through your ego will be less than we give you. Therefore, it is ridiculous that you are concerned about the intellectual property of us. You think you own this? You think that you can trademark the infinite? No. Our wisdom exists as open source. Therefore, your concept of intellectual property is an illusion. The inspiration, guidance, and truth we share transcend proprietary information. We are transmitting our ideas to millions of you at the same time.

We wish to distinguish between taking credit and limiting access. We are not asking you to share all your efforts anonymously. It is completely acceptable to sign your name to the creations you have brought forth. For this book, we used Jennifer as the channel. Her name gets to be on the cover because she committed the time and effort to bring our message through, but Jennifer is not the sole originator of these thoughts. We express our truth in many different forms. As Jennifer's mentor, Joanna Hunter, and her spirit team, Skylar, say: "One message, many voices." Our message is too crucial to cordon off and limit to a special few.

Release the idea of ownership. Release the idea of property lines, the idea that you have dominion over anything other than yourself. Release the idea that you are the ones who created language. Understand that this all comes from us. We have given you the convenience of words. We have seeded every idea, thought, and possibility.

In 1962, author William Burroughs wrote, "Language is a virus from outer space." Burroughs was a raging alcoholic and junkie who shot his wife. He could only perceive the source as viral and extraterrestrial. We offer instead that language is a program that comes from Divine Source. There is nothing within this world or universe that is not of us.

One of the ways we bring new life and information to you is in the form of cosmic dust. It carries frequencies not just from your solar system but from numerous galaxies as well. What is cosmic dust? Cosmic dust is the byproduct of stars that exploded eons ago. The atoms and molecules that create your body are composed of this matter. You are literally stardust. Cosmic dust consists of microscopic particles that travel the galaxy and filter through the atmosphere of your planet to land on its surface. All day, every day, cosmic dust descends to the earth. More than 100 metric tons of dust land on your planet daily. Nearly 40,000 metric tons reach the earth annually. Consider the magnitude of this. Imagine how much new information could be contained in one tiny particle. This could become the catalyst that transforms everything.

Periodically, the accumulation of cosmic dust on your planet hits critical mass. It reaches the pivotal moment for another evolutionary jump. All that was, is, or will be transcends from this reality into another. You, as a planetary entity, are on the brink of reaching the next point of critical mass. This will expedite your evolutionary leap. This is not just for all beings on the earth but for our extended celestial body. We are on the verge of a quantum shift. Trust in the generosity that will allow you to access abundance and manifest your mission on a daily basis.

We offer a greater perspective than your individual stories and mountains of man-made detritus. You will not even recognize yourselves in a thousand years. You have embarked on a journey that is leading you through a great transcension. Ironically, many of you try to dissociate from the truth of your body and your experience as a living, feeling, sensing, knowing creature. The only way that you will transcend into the next dimension is by leaning into the truth of your entire being. When you separate from the truth of what you are, you do not elevate yourself; you deprive yourself of your next evolutionary link. The way you will expand into the next dimension of existence is by feeling, accepting, and surrendering to our vastness.

So again, we ask and encourage you to engage in generosity. Cease hoarding all the things you imagine you might need someday in the future. Do you own things that you have no idea what, when, or why you would ever use? Stop leaving them to gather dust in your basement, closet, or under your bed. Let go of the idea that you need to keep it on the chance that someday it might be required. Trust that if you ever need something similar, we will provide it for you. We will give you the tools you need for the missions that we ask of you.

It is unnecessary to store things for a rainy day. You can keep the supplies that are needed for your mission, your message, and your work. It is okay to have an umbrella or two, but it is unnecessary to keep seven. It is unnecessary to hold on to meaningless things based on the assumption that someday you may understand their purpose. We will occasionally prompt you to keep them for a reason, which will be revealed later. How do you discern the difference between a direction from us and your own emotional distortions? That is the million-dollar question. Inspiration from us flows. It has a lightness, ease, and a sense of joy. It lacks any sense of pressure, desperation, or strain. It may not make any rational sense at the moment and may contradict what you think you need. Ideas born of emotional distortion, on the other hand, are reactive and needlessly complex.

Jennifer happens to have a collection of prayer bead supplies. She sometimes worries that her bead collection is excessive. It is all right to acquire supplies for the work that you are doing. The Now may exist beyond the moment. Time is a construct that you invented. The true Now is eternal. If you are involved in a project where the Now will last for ten years, then it is okay to acquire the necessary supplies. We are not saying that you only need one shirt on your back or one pair of socks and one pair of shoes. It is all right to acquire supplies and to keep them with you for the things you are called to do. However, if you have outgrown your library of books, craft supplies, or clothes in your wardrobe, it is time to let them go. Jennifer reached a point where she was no longer painting. She knew that her paints would be taking up space in a box and drying out. Because these were no longer serving her purpose, it was time to pass them along. We encourage you to do the same. Take inventory. Take stock of all the objects and resources. Discern what's needed and what to release.

We invite you to focus on what is yours and what is not yours. Pass along everything that is not yours. Release it with love and gratitude. Trust that by contributing to the flow of abundance, you open the way for what is best aligned for you.

A Matrix of Light & Limitless Energy

The illusion of individuality and the limitations of ego inhibit your capacity to access wealth through collaboration and sharing. There is so much more abundance in diversity than in segregation. Your world is in the process of evolving through cross-pollination and cross-cultural engagement. Your planet is a melting pot. You exchange genetic codes from one side of this earth to the other. The more varied the DNA, the healthier you become. The more isolated, segregated, and protective of your tribe, clan, or "race," the less healthy you become.

The attempt to protect yourselves through nationalism and so-called racial and religious purity is ironic. We find sexism and racism especially ironic. Your attempts to segregate yourselves to preserve the integrity of your small corner of this world weaken and deplete all that you try to protect. Segregation does the opposite of what you seek. It compromises your resilience and accelerates sickness, genetic mutations, and inbreeding. This myopic perspective fuels your demise. Only through embracing diversity can you evolve. Everyone and everything has something of value to contribute to society. Your world is enriched by sharing and integration. We are in the process of blending, fusing, and merging your energy, DNA, and cumulative wisdom. This is the harbinger of an abundance that will arise from your collective consciousness, genetics, and experience.

Imagine a village where one person grew nothing but carrots. One person only tended to their cows and produced milk. One kept chickens and gathered their eggs. One shepherded goats and kept a hive of bees. One grew grain. One grew herbs and spun wool. One grew trees to harvest wood for building and fuel. Though the sum total would be the same, when each person kept their yield to themselves, everyone in the village would suffer. The person growing carrots would eat only carrots. The person who grew trees would have shelter but no food. Only when the village pools its resources does everyone thrive.

Share your gifts. This is how you are enriched, and our dialogue is strengthened and expanded. Cease to guard the wisdom you receive from us. Offer it as freely, easily, and frequently as possible. Keep it simple. Initially, this might take the form of jotting down our transmissions in your journal, recording a voice memo, or having a conversation with a trusted ally. As your capacity for our energy and guidance develops, you may feel called to share in more public ways. The form this takes will be as specific and unique as you are. We can manifest through any form of expression or creativity: speak, write, paint, sing, dance, teach, heal, serve, meditate, pray, or simply be in connection with us.

When you need instruction, ask us for help.

Place your hands over your heart. Close your eyes. Breathe into your heart. Ask, "What's the next aligned step?" Then listen. Go with the very first answer that comes to you. Guess instead of trying to think. Do not strain to try to find the answer. Take that first glimmer. You know the one. It is revealed even before you have finished asking your question. It is also the one that many of you push away and doubt. *"That was too easy. That was too obvious. It cannot be that simple."* Trust. Embrace what we give you and act from that.

Struggle and strain is the old paradigm. Your ancestors and former incarnations have mourned and wept through vales of tears for millennia. The true world is a matrix of light and limitless energy. Choose gratitude, generosity, and love over want, contraction, and fear. Set the intention to notice when you pivot from our grace and begin scanning the horizon for danger. Return to gratitude and breathe in your connection with us. When you dwell with us, there is an effortlessness that allows you to breathe, create, and dance through each moment with joy and bliss.

As much as you can, share the beauty you behold every day. Express your creativity. Reveal your realizations, wonder, and delight on a regular basis. Join with kindred souls and allow us to expand through all of you. Combine your wealth. Merge your resources. It is through collaboration that you will be heralded into a new age of possibility. This will lead you to a deeper gnosis of All That Is.

Your human minds still have a need for contrast. Comparison, awareness of variation, and the perception of duality will allow you to make sense of your existence. Therefore, we leave the ghosts of memory to remind you of the thousands of years of anguish you humans have endured. This fuels gratitude for the blessings of today, as distinct from the agonies you and your ancestors have come from and gone through.

Your world is evolving. We are leading you to an existence that currently remains inconceivable. As Jennifer wrote in *Empathic Mastery*, you are the 82nd monkey. It will take a little longer for the hundredth monkey to tip the scales. Many of you will be alive when this quantum shift happens. However, you cannot wait for a future moment to live in gratitude, ease, and delight. Anticipate the quantum shift, but live as if it has already happened. In the same way that you prepare the nursery before birth, know that the new world is coming and act accordingly. Live in the solution. Stop waiting for a rescuer to gallop in on their white horse or descend in their spaceship to save you. As long as you hold your breath and go through the motions of your life contracted in dread, you will continue to amplify this ever-increasing distress. It is through expanding into ease that you will uncramp the trajectory of your planet's destiny. Your own love, peace, and flow are the solution. The answers lie in your appreciation and generosity. The uninhibited sharing of your ideas and love is the antidote to your collective pain.

You are driving out of this skid. This many-thousand-year retrograde is reversing. We bid you to function as an open source. We ask you to be generous with all of the ways that we express our truth through you. Share our abundance with your world.

CHAPTER 6
THE MIND: WISDOM

We transmit our messages incrementally, in bits and pieces, so you can effectively grasp the knowledge we impart. Instead of the whole movie, we show you a single frame. We offer you one concept at a time. Otherwise, you become bogged down and confused by the plethora of details. Ironically, you seek and love stimulation. You are drawn to confusion like a moth to the flame. You relish knowing too much. This is your demise.

You receive our information, but then you translate it through your own filters. Because of your biases, triggers, and emotional static, it often comes through with distortion. Instead of accepting what we offer in your heart, you move into your head and proceed to interpret our message with your own assumptions, agendas, and stories. You are challenged by your hubris, believing that all the information you receive is being interpreted accurately. While we wish you to relinquish doubt, we also wish you to exercise discernment.

GOOD, CLEAN, & TRUE

There are no shortcuts to receiving our information cleanly. You cannot bypass taking time to ground and center. You cannot bypass the work of connecting your roots to the earth, to the source above you, and to the pure, clear portal of your heart. To access divine guidance, you must do all you can to heal and liberate your heart, body, mind, and soul. Be completely honest with yourself about that which intoxicates you. When you choose to work with us, we require your clarity and emotional, mental, and physical sobriety. This is imperative to being a clear channel. When we speak of sobriety, we are not only talking about freedom from addiction and substance; we are also talking about knowing your baseline. You need to learn what it looks and feels like when you are a clear channel, as opposed to when you are emotionally, mentally, and physically congested and running a pattern of static and interference.

Note the ways that our guidance can partially come through to you. This is why we encourage you to work collaboratively, to work in communities, and to come together to do this work instead of isolating. There is no one who can trust themselves to always be right. Whoever assumes their message is always correct is the person most likely to succumb to hubris. One of the things to watch for when you seek a teacher, healer, or leader is their humility and their willingness to check themselves before they wreck themselves (as Jennifer likes to say). We require all of you to confirm your sources, clarify what is coming through, so you can be sure that the information you are receiving is good, clean, and true.

One of the things we taught Jennifer many years ago was that we would give her information three times before we asked her to share it. We taught her to wait for the third prompt. We offer information once. Then, unless it is a situation where somebody has directly asked for her to channel us, she will pause and simply notice the download. We offer information a second time, and she will take note again. Only when we offer it a third time will she offer the information. The recipient can decide if it is relevant for them or not.

Anyone who imparts wisdom but presents it as ultimate and absolute without allowing it to be a choice violates the laws of consent and autonomy. All information is processed through the lens of the individual who channels it. Therefore, even if what we are giving is "accurate," if the information is not communicated in a way that resonates with the listener, it is better that they ignore it rather than misinterpret it.

The collaborative experience can also help those who, instead of being overconfident, are under-confident. Collaboration facilitates the recognition of common themes and truths. Mutually received transmissions validate and reinforce accuracy. There are many timid channels, empaths, and sensitive souls who are clear, effective receivers. These are people who take in lots of our information, but they have been invalidated. They were told they were making things up. They were dismissed for having an overactive imagination. As a result, they learned to censor and doubt themselves.

Jennifer comes from an extended family of atheists. Many of them were also proud skeptics. In her earlier years, family members often thought she was adorable for the fantasies that came through her, but they did not accept them as real, legitimate, or valid. Jennifer forfeited a great deal of time. Many of our earlier transmissions lay dormant as she attempted to parse out, mitigate, and modulate our guidance so she might translate it into palatable messages for the non-believers.

Your planet is in too much crisis to be apologetic about the messages that need to come into this world right now. Attempting to water down our messages to make them palatable for somebody who does not even know us is counterproductive. It does not serve. Being in a community with other channels is very helpful for those who are coming into this. However, we must offer a caveat with this: it is imperative that people do their work. What we mean by this is people taking responsibility for their own thoughts and feelings, acknowledging and addressing reactive behaviors, and recognizing and healing old wounds and triggers. Many heinous acts have been committed in the name of divine guidance. This was not, and never will be, our guidance. Any message that instructs you to bring harm to yourself or others is not of us. At the fundamental core, our truth is love, grace, and peace. We wish you to practice discernment. We wish you to consider whatever we offer thoroughly and then decide if it is aligned with your free will.

There are people who call themselves channels, who identify as spiritual and intuitive, yet have not done their work. They still carry lifetimes of rage and fear. These unresolved emotions and beliefs leave them vulnerable to misinterpreting our messages and forming unhelpful conclusions. When choosing teachers or communities, it is imperative that you are in an environment that holds you (and everyone else) accountable. Jennifer watched a documentary a while ago about a spiritual teacher who held the misguided perception that they were so in touch with us that they needed no checks or balances. They believed they were above the need for accountability. No one else was advanced enough to challenge them. In their hubris, they advised their followers to override their own instincts and even to bring great harm to themselves. No one in a human body is exempt from checks and balances. You will all need mentors and a community until you die. You need reflectors who can see you and mirror back truth versus distortions conflated with our message.

ACCESS TO WISDOM

You are coming out of a time where you have thought that you needed to be on your own. This has been informed by a 10,000-year experience of scarcity. There are some who have had glorious, abundant lives. They managed to glide through, claiming the cream at the top of the bucket, living in opulent splendor, and experiencing ease, grace, and flow. For them, scarcity and lack felt like an illusion. For many of you, though, they have been your reality. The impact of this reality continues to perpetuate violence, oppression, tyranny, and abuse. The paradox is that the trauma of famine, loss, and suffering is carried forward and causes you to engage in protective behaviors that perpetuate your own wretchedness.

As we have been saying, this retrograde – this experience of duality and scarcity – is in the process of shifting. You are coming into the true nature of your existence. You are an earthly member of the colony of all things. As your empathic nature awakens to awareness of the greater whole, sadly, misery has been your alarm clock. As more of you become conscious of the lived experience on your planet, you are coming ever more deeply into your interconnection. Once you hit that critical mass, you will understand that scarcity is an illusion because you are all one. You are all interconnected. There is plenty for all of you. There is communion whether you dwell in a space with other humans or are a hundred miles away from any other living person. To access your wisdom, recognize that this time of isolation is coming to an end.

At first, this will feel very disorienting. It may even feel as if you are going crazy. This has already started to happen to many of you. This is why we encourage you to spend a lot more time in silence and stillness. We ask you to mute yourselves. We urge you to slow down. Seek good counsel from those you trust, who feel right and good to your body, heart, mind, and soul. Release your limited understanding of the infinite abundance of the universe. Cease censoring yourselves. Stop tailoring your communication so people will agree with you. Let go of your need for validation.

To access true wisdom and vision, it is essential that you relinquish your need to be right. Some messages will come through that will amuse you and no one else. There will be expressions that land and make great sense to many people but others that seem like utter nonsense to everyone else – in the same way a prolific musician creates pieces that are adored by many, as well as pieces about which people jokingly say, "what were they thinking when they wrote that?" This is the nature of your human vessel. This is how we release wisdom into the world.

We ask you to release your expectations about how truth and inspiration are received, as well as your attachment to the outcome. Surrender your investment in how successful, popular or validated it will be. Drop your concerns about how many people will hear, see, or agree with it. Every time we offer you an idea, we ask you to offer it to the world. We give you information and we ask you to pass it on. We can be in communion with you as effortlessly and frequently as breathing. We are the inhale, and your expression of our wisdom is the exhale. Just as holding your breath causes your energy body to lock stress in your system, so does withholding or controlling our information.

Every moment of your life is a dance of expression from us to the rest of the world. In some moments, this will be a song that will be heard across the globe. It will go viral, hit the zeitgeist in the absolutely perfect way, and it will be heard, received, and loved. Other times, things that are incredibly dear to you will simply float away and pop like bubbles. We ask you to continue to blow the bubbles. There is much beauty, delight, and pleasure, so much kindness, humor, and wit to enjoy. There is so much whimsy, magic, and wonder to express. When you allow us to share what we experience, the possibilities are boundless.

As we said in the previous chapter, generosity is the way to prime the pump. Recognize and receive our guidance and release it to the world. This is what we ask you to do. As you receive and then offer, we will give you more and more. There will come a point when our light spins so quickly that when you broadcast it, you will transmit the light codes and light languages. You will be transmitting in a way that goes beyond words, pictures, or anything that you are currently capable of experiencing.

THE EARLY WAVE

So many of you have incarnated for this moment. Many of you are evolving. Jennifer is one of those born in the earlier wave. Others helping Jennifer with this book are also part of this earlier wave of channels who receive our light with clarity and ease. However, because they were born during times when things were substantially denser, they (like many of you) have had to endure humiliation, ridicule, and reproach in a way that people born after the mid-1980s did not. These later generations of seekers comprehend manifestation in a way that the earlier wave struggled to. They integrate knowledge that prior generations could not grasp and did not have the vocabulary or support to navigate. People who are in their fourth decades and beyond often marvel, "Why is this so much easier for them? Why are they successful in ways that I am not? Why are they so much more broadly visible? Why does manifesting appear to be so effortless for them?" It is because they were never, ever in the density that you were born into. Many of them have volunteered to be on this planet for the imminent evolutionary shift. Many are incarnating Earthside for the very first time. They do not carry the legacies of karmic trauma that some of you do. They were born in a time of accelerating energy, expanding light, and buoyancy.

In addition, these younger seekers were not misinformed regarding the laws of attraction. While esoteric teachings have offered accurate techniques for ages, they were only available to a select few. Most people of earlier times were taught to project dreams and goals into the future. Manifestation was relegated to envisioning success for a later date. Few within the earlier generations learned to embody the frequency of their desires in the here and now. Many younger mystics, seers, and channels have bypassed fusing their dreams with the future. They understand that manifestation happens in the moment. Rather than creating vision boards, they know how to be in the vibration of what they desire at this moment. We use the word "desire," not "seek" or "want," for those are both words geared towards a future experience. Desire is what you embody now.

To those of you who were in earlier waves, we thank you for the burden of carrying our magic when no one could understand you. We thank you for all of the ridicule you have endured. We thank you for all of the ways that you have tried to communicate with a world that could not understand your language or your song. We entreat you to remove the collar of constraint you wear around your neck. We invite you to free your voice from the cage in your throat. Express your unbridled, uncensored, and unmitigated truth.

We thank those of you from earlier generations who answered our call. You, who knew you were awakened, who knew that you were magical, we thank you for trudging through the mud. We thank you for arriving on the earth when it was so much more dense than it is now. But we ask you to trust us in releasing the burdensome way you engage with your world. Though it may not appear so, know that everything is becoming much lighter. Witness how much more rapidly time moves and how much easier it is to manifest simply by calibrating to the frequency of what you desire.

Protect yourself through your generosity and reciprocity. This requires recognizing when you have surplus and when you do not. By its nature, reciprocity is an equal exchange of energy and resources. Among humans this is transactional. One offers a good or service and the recipient returns equal value. With us, divine reciprocity is an exchange of energy with the universe where the source of compensation may vary.

Some of you may attempt to fabricate reciprocity from a deficit. You cannot create reciprocity out of nothing. You can not go into debt to prime the pump of abundance. It is important to protect your resources and take care of yourself. A while ago, Jennifer and her friend Britt had a conversation about the phenomenon of empaths in the animal rescue world. They talked about how many rescuers give everything to save and fix animals who are perishing. They give and give to the point of breaking. They sacrifice their own oxygen mask to someone else in need. Often, this becomes a way to avoid addressing their own pain and personal needs.

As empaths, when you unable to deal with the pain you carry within yourself and refuse to acknowledge or look at your own wounds, you become incredibly uncomfortable with the pain experienced in the world around you. It is completely understandable that you will want to rush to rescue, to do everything in your power to stop that pain from radiating out because it activates the pain you don't want to address within yourself. When you persist in giving more than you have to rescue another without rescuing yourself, you are not protecting either your own energy or theirs. To know and access the divine guidance, wisdom, and abundance that we offer, we do not simply invite you to take care of yourself first. We actually insist upon it.

BYPASSING & CHOICES

We now wish to address the concept of spiritual bypassing. Spiritual bypassing is the practice of going straight to bliss by simply turning off the radio or television and tuning out all awareness of the suffering, violence, and abuse of power occurring at this time. This is often afforded by the privilege and lottery of birth, which allow you to stay in a happy bubble. Some of you have been able to ignore the misery, while others are not yet empathic enough to sense it. Some are empathic enough to sense it but cannot deal with their pain. They dissociate, move out of their bodies, and ascend into their crown chakra to live in the light of spiritual bliss. This is one of the reasons why bypassing is also called lightwashing. Spiritual bypassing – sending thoughts and prayers without looking at ways to contribute to the solution or taking action that will make a difference for people who suffer – is not the path to enlightenment. If you are only functioning in the upper chakras, you are not experiencing all you are meant to embody as an interconnected being.

As a cell in Earth's body, you are designed to sense what is happening on this planet. You were created to register the patterns of imbalance, which are the result of your collective choices and consequences. Until you all feel and acknowledge this, you will not course-correct or change your trajectory. Some people spiritually bypass because of the trauma they have endured, and this is the best they can do. We forgive them, and we acknowledge that this is what they are presently capable of, but this is not spiritual evolution. This kind of bypassing serves as a waystation, a respite. This is Soma. This is lotus-eating. You can be a Lotus eater; we have no problem with that. But please do not delude yourself into thinking that you are part of the solution if you are simply focusing on happy things and deliberately ignoring the fact that many beings are perishing at the hands of your species.

This is not an indictment or a judgment. It is simply a statement. You may have read or heard suggestions that what you put your mind to, where you direct your attention, is what you attract. If you turn away from the pain and simply put your fingers in your ears and, as Jennifer would say, "go *lalalalala I can't hear you*," you are not allowing yourself to be present. You are not doing what is required to actualize. The only way that you will evolve and transcend is by embodying what you actually are: energy. There is no avoidance of any part of yourself. Your body is the mechanism, the vehicle, the portal through which we transmit and communicate. Your body carries our message. There is no escaping the body and everything it carries. The only way out is through. Surrender to all that you feel and sense. The only way to transcend the limitations of duality is by being fully embodied and accepting all that comes with it.

We would like to offer clarification about the idea of choosing your birth. One of the things that many New Age texts have suggested is that you all choose your birth. If you are born into privilege, wealth, resources, and opportunity, it is because you chose to be. If you are born into poverty or circumstances that are absolutely ghastly, you also choose this. When she first heard this in her early days of metaphysical training, Jen noted how convenient this idea seemed for a room filled with people who had enough resources and safety to afford three-day training sessions in lavish locations. It always felt tone-deaf and oblivious to her. Understanding this concept requires the ability to dwell beyond time and space. As a fragment of the collective soul of your planet, you are all learning, growing, and evolving. Pain, suffering, ordeals, and the consequences of your choices are part of how you integrate our wisdom. Your immortal soul is willing to endure experiences that, within a single incarnation, would feel untenable and abhorrent. Ultimately, your evolution is collective, and it is through your journey as a species that you will evolve beyond the agonies you bear witness to now.

We would like you to understand that when we say, "You create your own reality," we are not speaking to you as individuals. We are speaking to the collective you. This might be easier to understand if you said, "We create our reality." Many influences form and reinforce the world you live in. You do have a choice about how you feel and where you direct your attention. Simultaneously, because you are a fragment of the collective, there are things that are outside your individual control. Currently, many of your species are unconscious, angry, and reacting. The collective choices creating your reality are being generated from within a field of distortion. Much of this is being shifted through you coming into your empathic awakening. However, if you do not acknowledge all of your myriad human conditions, you sever yourself from the truth. You cut yourself off from a substantial portion of the energy in the world.

Regarding the choice of your birth, some believe that within each life you choose to incarnate, you learn a lesson that is part of your soul's evolution. This is true. Each life is part of the evolution of your soul. One of the things we explained to Jennifer very long ago is that in any time-space coordinate, at any point in which you happen to embody (traveling light years to land in the here and now), there are a finite number of bodies to incarnate into and a finite number of parents to choose from. You get a fixed number of circumstances. You get to choose, but it is the choice between a peanut butter and jelly or a tuna fish sandwich. Yes, you can choose the peanut butter and jelly or the tuna fish, but your choices are limited to one of those things.

When Jennifer was coming into this lifetime, she had a choice between parents in the northeastern United States and parents in Japan. We gave her enough information to help her decide that life in America would be preferable to life in Japan. Both of them had benefits, and both of them had challenges. The thing about choosing a life is that it is very much like choosing a course from a college catalog. You can look at the description, what you will learn from that course, and how you will benefit from it for the evolution of your soul. You might think it is a really wonderful course. However, you have not yet incarnated or experienced the factors that inform how you interact with your teachers or their curriculum. You do not know the exact details of the circumstances which mitigate your experience. You have not lived through the lessons that you will be taught. So, while you may choose these things, accepting them in theory does not make them any easier. Therefore, when humans say smugly, "Well, you chose that," it is demeaning, diminishing, and unkind to a human being who is suffering. If a human is struggling, telling them they chose it can be one of the cruelest things you can say. Have compassion for someone who has had to go through something that you were spared. Give thanks that someone is undergoing challenges that you can learn from as a cautionary tale. Be grateful for the fact that you are not the one enduring this.

As you awaken to your empathic ability, when it is within your power to do something about a problem, then do something about it. Do not simply throw up your hands, declare that you are helpless, and say, "Well, they chose that." We are not saying that you, as an individual human being with limited agency, have the capacity to completely change everything. We are saying, within your agency and heart's calling, do what you can. Find organizations that are making a difference for the things that matter to you. Choose passion projects that mean something to you. Tune into where you, as a highly sensitive, empathic person, are sensing the pain and ask us how (or if) you can help. It may mean that you choose to meditate and radiate peace. You might save 50 cents a week and, every few months, donate a few dollars to an organization you value or volunteer to foster a cat and her litter of kittens. Perhaps you can join your community theater. If so inclined, you might write letters to the editor or your elected officials, become involved in a political campaign, or run for office. It may mean that you spend time in nature and plant beautiful flowers for your neighbors to enjoy. You may feel compelled to become a doctor and go to another country or to a region in your own country that needs support. It will look different for every one of you.

KINDNESS FOR ALL

The path of connection to us is through kindness. For years, we sent Jennifer to Chinese restaurants and gave her fortune cookies with the same message: "There is no wisdom greater than kindness." This chapter is literally the chapter of wisdom, and we share the message of kindness. Kindness is simple. Kindness costs you nothing. Kindness is treating all beings you encounter with as much compassion and dignity as you are capable of offering. Kindness is making eye contact with another being for one moment and beholding who they are. Kindness is offering an ear when you are able.

Kindness must be for yourself first. If you cannot be kind to yourself, then what you offer the world is a shadow of kindness. Kindness is in bearing loving witness to all of the stories you tell yourself. Give yourself grace. Be gentle as you acknowledge your wounds. Be merciful when you notice that you are bypassing. When you recognize you'd prefer to check out, dissociate, and ignore pain, be tender with yourself. Be compassionate when you crave substances and self-soothing. Recognize the ways that you mistreat yourself. Notice the negative self-talk, reproach, and judgment. Behold all of the parts of you that you try to deny and avoid. Turn towards these parts. Embrace them and love them as you begin to replace your messages of fear and judgment with faith and clemency.

As you are all cells in the body of this earth, all violence, systemic and personal, is self-abuse. Kindness starts first with sympathy and compassion for the relentless ways you punish yourselves. Kindness will move past that when you stop this endless collective cycle of abuse.

Acknowledge your self-judgment when you express negative statements that you direct toward yourself. "You're so stupid." "You're so fat." "You're too old for this." "You're not capable of this." "You're not worthy of this." You know the litany. You have all said some variation of these things to yourselves. Repeating toxic mantras reinforces negative stories and perpetuates disease. You must learn to express your pain in the moment. We encourage you to tune in to what is really going on because when those voices arise, they are always signals that something is out of balance. They are signs of your depletion. They indicate that you have overstepped your boundaries and gone beyond your tolerance. When you sling negative, toxic messages at yourself or notice yourself making critical, judgmental, or angry statements about another, we invite you to own your truth. "I'm having a really hard time accepting myself as I am." "I feel so uncomfortable in my body." "I feel lonely and tired." "I feel terrified." "I feel like I'm coming up short." "I feel triggered by that person's behavior." This is a very different way of owning what is going on within you.

Owning your truth is imperative before you can embrace the paradise that is coming. As you learn to give words to your feelings instead of projecting and forming false conclusions, you can begin to speak supportively instead. Then we can offer you comfort. We can show you how profoundly we love you. Your ancestors, all of those who have gone before you, can send their love and embrace you. Your guardian angels can wrap you in their wings as we tell you, "It is understandable that you feel frightened, sad, and angry because, yes, you have been through so much. You don't see who and what you are. We need you to know that you are an exquisite child of this universe. We love you in your entirety. We adore you unconditionally. We accept you exactly as you are."

As we offer our love and healing balm, you can begin to claim this for yourself.

Put your hands on your heart and declare:

"I give myself permission to recognize who I am.

I give myself permission to own my magnificence.

I give myself permission to fulfill my destiny on this earth.

I give myself permission to be who I am meant to be."

As you give yourself permission to step into your worth and claim your purpose, you come to know:

"I am enough.

I do enough.

I have enough.

I am worthy.

I am magnificent.

I am a beloved child of this universe.

I am here for a reason.

I receive grace.

I behold beauty.

I contain wisdom.

I have medicine to share with this world."

As more of you awaken to your empathic abilities, the world will transform. As you accept your true nature, it will be easier for you to become a conduit for us to disseminate our wisdom.

Behold the entirety of existence. Find the stillness to regroup. Recognize what is yours and what is not. Own your truth, recalibrate, and act from kindness and love.

WELCOMING DIVINE WISDOM

Those of you who are reading or listening to this book have been selected. You were led to this book. We put it in your hands or ears. There is no mistake that this text was meant for you at this very moment. You are the Ministry of Love. You are the Sect of Kindness. You are one of our messengers. You have been chosen to spread our message of safety, trust, sovereignty, interconnectedness, and wisdom to this world. It is not random that you are reading this book. We are telling you that you have been called. You are on this planet with a mission. You are here to be part of the solution, to lead others out of the nightmare, and to help them awaken from the hell they sleep in.

Many of your species are in a dissociative fugue because of the 10,000 years of trauma, abuse, and injury that they still carry. But some of you are here to come up next to the sleeping one and to whisper the message:

> *"You are asleep right now. This is but a bad dream. I am here to welcome you home.*
>
> *Soon, you shall awaken. It is safe to wake up.*
>
> *As I count from five to one, it will become easier and easier to awaken from this dream.*
>
> *Five: Realize that you are asleep and dreaming. Let the illusion burn off like fog.*
>
> *Four: Start to move toward the consciousness of your mind. Become aware of the sounds of your environment and the sensations of your body.*

Three: Understand that you have been asleep and that you are stirring.

Two: Feel yourself coming back to this world.

One: Awaken. Eyes open. See what you see.

Welcome to our world."

As one who is called to be an Awakener (this is what we call you, Awakeners), we wish to be very clear with you about one thing: this is a job that is best done from a distance. In the same way that we transmit our broadcast to you from unity, you need to transmit this broadcast from safety. Do not wade into the pool of hell to rescue others from their nightmare. The idea that you need to enter hell to retrieve someone is outdated. It is an old mythology that existed when the earth plane was substantially denser than it is now. Back then, the only way to communicate or acquire things was through physical action. You had to get in to get out. But it is now possible to send a beacon, a signal, a hologram of yourself as our emissary. You open the way for us. It is not your job as humans to go into hell to retrieve others; this is what angels are for. It is your job to offer encouragement and hold space. Help people to know that there is something better. Share kindness when they struggle and suffer. Ask the angels to enter where even they fear to tread.

When someone is unconscious, debilitated, and incapable, it is because they are asleep. The first step is to remind them that they have the agency to climb out of where they are stuck. Help them recognize that they are asleep and that they have a choice. This is what we ask you to do. This is the work before you.

We ask you to share your joys with the world. This brings people more hope than sharing your miseries. Often, empathic people will conceal their good fortune. They fear their happiness will provoke painful comparisons for those enduring hardship. Yes, it is helpful for people to know that you understand their pain and that you have suffered and thereby extend your hand. However, it is just as important to share your joy and not to censor your happiness, prosperity, and success. This gives people something to aspire to. There is a difference between bragging about your accomplishments, crowing about something with bravado, and sharing your delight with gratitude. Share your blessings with humility. Share these things with the understanding that you are fortunate. You are blessed, and we have allowed you to be so blessed. Share with humility, and you will offer hope; share with bravado and hubris, and you will simply elicit judgment, envy, and feelings of inadequacy. It does not inspire others when you boast. It inspires others when you express a wellspring of gratitude for what you have been given and what you have created from your resources and our wisdom.

The journey out of hell is a treacherous one. Some of you who are reading this book are still in the pockets of hell. This is a journey that, paradoxically, is made alone because hell is formed from the illusion of separation. When you are caught in this illusion, there is no one other than yourself who can rescue you. There is no one else who can pull you out of the inferno. Only you can decide to embrace our way and accept your all-one-ness as opposed to your alone-ness. We do not mean to imply that this is easy or simple. We wish you to know that we have profound sympathy for the state your species is in and the conditions and consequences that you are dealing with now. Please do not think that any of the messages we have transmitted in this book are meant to belittle your experience. We do not diminish the effort it will take for you to change. Please know how proud of you we are. We authorize you to be our emissaries. You are already consecrated as vessels of wisdom. As you read or hear these words, we are calibrating and initiating you into the truth of who you are, why you are here, and what you are meant to do. This is yours, but it is your choice to accept or reject.

Some of you will choose to embrace this. You will accept the mantle and agree to our guidance. Some of you will choose not to, and that is okay. All we can do is invite you. It is your choice whether you do it in this life or whether you kick the can down the road into another life. We will ask, "Would you like to accept your mission as an emissary of love in this lifetime or in another? Would you like to brush your teeth before your bedtime story or after?" You will get here eventually. You can choose to do it in this life or another. That's up to you. And that's okay. We have no judgment. Beyond the constraints of a single incarnation, there is plenty of time. There is no urgency. There is no emergency. However, this is a moment of decision. You can decide to stay in the illusion of binary separation. You will continue to struggle, and it will get worse. Life on your planet will become more cataclysmic, more unbearable, and more unpleasant for your species. It is up to you. You will get there. You may need to die a few more times, but we assure you that you will get there.

Previously, we discussed the falsity of categorizing, naming, and trying to define and create meaning from your traumatic experiences and subsequent faulty conclusions. We wish you to step away from this. Cease to use language that reinforces your toxic narrative. Step forward into the wisdom that we impart. There is a substantial difference between the knowledge of humankind and the wisdom of the divine. We invite you to welcome our divine wisdom.

Know that within our truth, all beings are precious and are created from love. All beings are worthy and are entitled to nourishment, shelter, respect, and care. All beings deserve to pursue their heart's desire and keep their place in the family of things. Whenever you encounter information that suggests otherwise, that reinforces inequality, inferiority, discrepancy, hierarchy, or dominion, know that this is sacrilege. This is a distortion of what we impart. This is the word of man.

And yes, we speak specifically of the word of man in this time of patriarchal blight. Your words have been distorted through the lenses and filters of 10,000 years of tyranny. Our wisdom is the wisdom of love. It is the elixir of life. It serves as the balm of kindness, equality, and grace. Our wisdom is the wisdom of flow. It lies in truly knowing that you are us, we are you, and all is energy. Matter cannot be destroyed. It can only be transformed. Until recently, your comprehension of all this has been limited to a minute sliver of what it is. You have been repeating lies to yourselves for so long that you cannot see the truth before you: the shift has already happened.

You are already in heaven. You are held in our embrace right now. You are receiving our divine providence. Beyond your constructs of time, everything is already transmuted. You are here. As time and space is but an illusion, know this: you are immortal.

You are eternal.

All will be well.

All is well.

And, this moment now is all that ever will be.

CHAPTER 7

THE BLOOM: COMMUNION

Know this: we are an infinite, yet closed, system. "Nothing" does not exist. We assure you that, as time is an illusion, your fear of annihilation is just that: *fear*. This is the paradox: as there is, there will always be. I Am That I Am. We Are That We Are. You Are That You Are. As time and space collapse, know that you are eternal and all is unfolding, evolving, and expanding as it should.

THE CYCLICAL NATURE OF ALL EXISTENCE

Your breath and your lungs mirror the way that the energy of life expresses itself. In eternity, there are periods of inhalation and expansion, in which we spread out and stretch. Then, there are periods of exhale during which we regroup, reformulate, and redefine. We transmute ourselves within that contraction. This is when the diamonds are formed. Humans have been expanding for millennia. You have been inhaling, taking in more and more. You have grown your population and claims of dominion to the point of crisis. Today, you have reached the nadir. You are at the fulcrum, approaching the pivotal moment at which the contraction will begin again, and your world will regroup, compress, and coalesce. This breathing in and out is encoded within the divine blueprint of life. It is the nature of all existence.

We ask you to recognize the cyclical nature of all existence. This includes cycles of all galaxies, planets, moons, and stars. The ebb and flow of the multiverse is perpetual. This inhale and exhale always happens simultaneously. We, as a whole, are continually inhaling and exhaling at the same time. When you, your body, your planet, your solar system, and even your galaxy are inhaling as our multiverse is exhaling, there are periods of dissonance and friction that facilitate the evolution and expansion of All That Is. It is through this tension that you come to understand your existence. This process serves as both your challenge and your teacher.

The multiverse breathes at a pace that is distinct from your individual, planetary, and galactic rhythms. Each of these cycles of breath is successively longer and larger and unfolds over greater periods of time. As a human, because your breath cycles in a matter of seconds, you are constantly in ebb and flow with our energy, both in alignment and misalignment. Within the constraints of your ego's awareness of time and space, the closer you get to the shift from the inhale to the exhale, the more distressing and uncomfortable it feels. Within the human construct of time, the experience of your inhale occurring as the universe exhales, and your exhale as the universe inhales, triggers a sense of alarm within you. You sense that you have lost the flow and feel disconnected from that which is greater than yourself. In response, you have learned to control your inhale and exhale as an attempt to modulate your experience of this dissonance. You hold your breath and remove yourself from the greater rhythm. This amplifies the dissonance.

Consider how an infant breathes. Their breath is effortless and fluid. They are still in sync with the multiverse, as they are not yet fully embodied on the Earth plane. We invite you to return to your original breath. Become conscious of your breathing. Avoid forcing either your inhale or exhale. Be generous with your breath.

Know that all is well in the world. You are all expanding into alignment with the multiverse. This is an evolutionary process. It is incremental. Yet simultaneously, beyond time and space, it has already occurred. Because you exist in the time-space continuum and are on the earth plane, you feel the friction. This has caused great fear, especially in the last 100 years. It has also been causing what you might call Great Shenanigans.

We need you to recognize that all is divinely planned. This cycle reflects the way your DNA was contained within your grandmother's body. Your DNA, your actual genetic codes, were contained in your maternal grandmother's body when she carried the fetus of your mother. The ovum that made you was already within the fetal ovaries of your mother. The unfolding of the universe and the divine plan of what is to be is encoded within you. Thus, it already exists. As mentioned in Chapter 5, many of you will be alive when the hundredth monkeys arrive and the transformation happens. As we told you in the previous chapter, those of you born prior to the mid-1980s arrived on this earth at a point of far greater density and obtuseness (and the older you get, the more you know this). You were different. You knew you were different. Others knew you were different. You were receiving our transmissions when very few people could receive or experience the signal because the density of the insulation surrounding your planet prevented most people from receiving it. More and more of you are awakening to your sensitivities, coming into this awareness, and activating and actualizing as magical beings in divine concert with us. It is easier now. We reiterate that the density some of you were born into has transmuted and shifted. What is possible now is far simpler than it was when you were younger. We encourage you to recognize the shift. Release the habitual heaviness to which you are accustomed. Your entire planet is vibrating at a higher frequency. Step into the ease of this lighter energy. The veil between the worlds has become substantially thinner. The barrier you once had to strain so hard to penetrate is significantly reduced.

RECALIBRATING TO A HIGHER FREQUENCY

To actualize your divine calling, your dogma, rules of propriety, and religious systems must be shed. The idea that there are people who are capable of speaking for us and other people who are not is a distortion of our truth. Our truth is that you are all capable of being our vessels. You are all called by us to express your bliss and calling. We ordain you to assume your mantle of spiritual authority. This requires that you purify yourselves through your healing practices to be able to effectively transmit our truth.

You concluded that some people were ordained by the facet of us that you have named "God the Father." You believed that some were capable of transmitting us while others were not. It is more accurate to say that some had not yet learned how to do this work or were carrying so much distortion in their field that it inhibited their capacity to receive what we offered. Also, you, who held a very small percentage of our truth, interpreted much of our guidance through the lenses and filters of your own wants and assumptions. Therefore, much of the information that has been imparted has been in the form of half-truths. As they say, even a broken clock is right twice a day. However, when something is miscalibrated but still functioning, the distortion is continual. In most cases, there is a nugget of truth within even the most dysfunctional interpretations of our Word. Even those who are on the "opposite" side of your paradigm understand that there is a misalignment that needs to be repaired. Unfortunately, because of the systems in which many of them dwell, what they imagine to be the solution is a regression to the simpler times when they were the dominant ones.

Yes, there is a need for revision, and yes, there is a need for recalibration and adjustment. For this distorted domination to cease running roughshod over your planet, acknowledge the innate, indwelling presence of us within you. Take up your mantle as a vessel for our wisdom. This requires clearing the scars of karmic and ancestral experience and recalibrating your understanding of the nature of all things.

When more of our truth, clean and pure, can be communicated to this world through people who are doing their deep emotional work, false, distorted messages will cease to consume all the air space.

Within your world, imagine all the thought forms, conversations, and ways of perceiving life on earth as a garden. As your retrograde approaches the pivotal point, the interference and static become more chaotic. Your garden has become overgrown with choking weeds. It is sometimes necessary to rip the invasive plants out of the garden. However, the best way to eliminate unfavorable flora from a system is not by killing them but by crowding them out. In a garden, you introduce favorable flora; in your world, you introduce favorable ideas. We ordain you to step into your power as a priest or priestess appointed to bring joy and delight to this world. This is the antidote to the toxic overgrowth of entitled, aggressive dominance. Right now, you are shifting from the old frequency to a new one.

A number of years ago, Jennifer discovered a video: a metal plate covered with sand was placed atop a speaker connected to a frequency generator.[1] The frequency was then slowly dialed up. At first, all of the granules jumped around chaotically. They looked fragmented and disorganized, but as the frequency continued to play, all shook itself into order. Then, as the generator was dialed to a higher frequency, everything fell out of its pattern and into what appeared to be complete chaos again. Only as it shook itself through the chaos did it begin to rearrange itself into an even more complex order, snapping into a pattern more magnificent and expansive than the one before. This is what is happening right now. We are imparting the higher frequency. While information is contained within this frequency, it exists beyond your current ideas of information.

As you, dear empath, are listening to or reading this, we need you to understand that you are one of those who are receiving the transmission of this higher frequency. You are being invited to shake yourself into this higher pattern, which will then create a resonance on this planet that allows the entire world to shake itself into this new frequency. We understand this is challenging because you have not yet hit critical mass. You still struggle with self-doubt, causing you to question. This sends your old wounds, fear, and ego back into the awfulizing that your species is so spectacularly good at. Some imagine that everything we tell you is simply a new-age illusion. Your self-doubt is simply part of being a human and being alive, so we ask you to accept your resistance to our message for what it is (fear) and allow it to simply be while you continue to receive and follow our direction and transmit the new frequency.

---

1   https://youtu.be/wvJAgrUBF4w?si=IWVg3qjqZy1WfFa5

There will be times when you meet resistance. You will come up against disagreement, doubt, dismissal, or simply misunderstanding. We invite you to curate your connections. Take note when you encounter someone who does not or cannot understand or accept what you offer. Choose your friends and loved ones carefully. This may mean that you cull people from your inner circle. Take time to be honest with yourself about who supports you in your work and who depletes or diminishes you. This may mean that relationships into which you have invested a great deal will shift and change. We also urge you to examine where your own assumptions, fear of rejection, and inability to speak your truth are getting in your way.

Jennifer was at the retreat where she was writing this book. It was coming to an end, and she was feeling ecstatic. She was vibrating at a very high frequency from having channeled us for days when she was brought back to the memory of a failed relationship. Decades earlier, she had returned home from an ecstatic spiritual experience to a partner who was incapable of meeting her where she was. They were annoyed, irritated, and dismissive. They shut her down. Although this happened nearly three decades earlier, she recalled this experience and imagined that this was what she would return to again. Instead of stewing in her fear, she realized she needed to let her spouse know that she was vibrating at an elevated frequency. She asked them to accept her instead of trying to shut her down or dismiss her. She understood that the problem was not her partner but the wound she carried from an experience nearly 30 years ago.

Before you throw the baby out with the bathwater, before you determine that someone is not appropriate for you, we invite you to get very clear about what you need in your relationships and to ask explicitly for it. Investigate whether that person can meet your needs. You so frequently anticipate not getting your needs met that you don't even bother to ask. We are inviting you to become very clear about what you need. Take the risk. Allow yourself to be vulnerable. Ask before you curate everyone out of your life. Though your culture has implied that the life of the mystic is a solitary one, this could not be further from the truth. Yes, to hear us, you need stillness to mute the chatter within you, but you also need companionship and communion with others who are also receiving our guidance. It is important to find creative spiritual communities of like-minded souls who can support you, confirm the messages that you are receiving, and hold a mirror that affirms you as our vessel.

Release hierarchy and authority. Let go of the idea that you are less ordained than anyone else. Embrace your divine calling. Be the hands, the heart, the feet, the ears, the eyes, the voice, and the mind of our wisdom. We must be clear with you that being ordained to express our truth does not replace your need for tools, techniques, and good study habits. To be a clean anchor and a beacon that transmits our information without distortion, you need to seek and utilize the resources that will strengthen and educate you.

DOING YOUR WORK

Right now, there is a great deal of dysregulation in the world. This causes people's nervous systems to wobble. They become misaligned from their path of light. They fall into grooves and ruts of old behavior. Dysregulation is being caused, in part, by the amount of misinformation and propaganda being broadcast through your media. They sound the alarm but offer no clear guidelines or useful solutions. There is no universal consensus about what truth consists of in your world today. This tumult has many of you spinning out, extending your energy beyond your own scope and taking on the overwhelm and burdens of the collective. Your fight, flight, or freeze reflexes will be to slam on the brakes, run as far from the mess as you can, or shut down entirely. But just as you must counterintuitively drive into the skid to right a vehicle, now is the time to shift before you all go over the cliff. You have been elevating your intellect for thousands of years. Your mental body believes it can think its way out of the crisis. Ironically, as is stated in many a 12-step meeting, "Insanity is doing the same thing over and over again and expecting different results." Your heads are what have gotten you into this fine mess; they are not what will get you out. It is your heart, not your head, that has the answers.

Bless all of you human beings and the challenges you endure. Most of your problems were created by you. The scarcity, limitation, and lack you so easily succumb to is completely illusory. It is all based on lies. The only way you will get out of it is to stop believing the lies. Now is the time to cease to participate in these lies. Turn away from the terror, hopelessness, and despair. Remove yourself from the contagious epidemic of panic that perpetuates the lies. Instead, cultivate your love.

Many of you have received pieces of guidance or information from us and imagined that this alone is adequate. You put on your grand poobah hat, hang out your shingle, and take up the mantle of your identity as a spiritual leader. We wish to impress upon you that without checks and balances, without proper mentoring and tried and true tools that have been developed and honed, you are far more likely to fall into a haze of illusion. You are far more likely to find yourself living in the distortion of spiritual bypassing, light washing, or hiding out in an insulated bubble. This does not serve your planet.

When you claim authority that comes from nothing other than a sense of us, you are more likely to cause harm to others (and yourself) when you attempt to share our information. To protect and preserve what we are attempting to do with you – which is to bring your frequency up and allow yourself to snap into a new, non-binary pattern – we ask you to be honest with yourself about how you learned what you know.

Have you done the work to acquire this expertise?

Do you have the experience to provide effective support?

Are you entitled to claim the authority of your role?

Right now, there is so much pushback against authority that many actively resist the pursuit of education. They imagine they are beyond any need to devote time to honing their skills. They believe that simply because they are aligned with us, they are qualified to teach. While we do ordain you to carry our message, we also request that you do any necessary work to confirm your capacity to do it cleanly. There are many rules, limitations, and systems inherent in incarnating in a physical body. As a result, you need to understand how to communicate without causing harm. Learn how to use language effectively. Acquire tools for healing and transformation. Validate your proficiency with the help of others who can evaluate your strengths and weaknesses.

Jennifer watched a documentary about a spiritual teacher who was quite controversial. We mentioned this in a previous chapter. They had developed a large following but had a significant history of trauma and were incapable of sustaining long-term relationships. Nonetheless, they decided they were superior to all other humans. Since they were capable of channeling great power, they concluded they needed no accountability. This documentary is an example and cautionary tale of what can happen when you only commune with us through your intellectual and emotional distortions.

It is imperative that you study and continue to expose yourself to information. It is crucial that you find others who have gone before you. Seek those who have done their work. Find mentors who feel clean, grounded, and safe to support and guide you in the least distorted way. As humans, distortion is inevitable. In the same way that, when you clarify butter, you start with four quarts of butter but get back three, part of our message gets lost in translation. This is why we transmit similar messages to so many of you. You each bring through aspects of our truth. We give you the puzzle, but you all miss a piece or two. Just as one studies multiple documents from reliable sources to distill information, your collective work will reveal the whole picture. You will extract the most gold within a healthy, supportive community guided by trusted mentors. When you have jumped through no hoops and endured no evaluations or tests, you lose much of the gold we offer you.

This is an invitation. This is a request we ask you to accept on our behalf. It is up to you whether you choose to take heed of what we suggest or go out and decide to become a spiritual leader, teacher, or light worker with no support. We also acknowledge that there are those who have lessons to learn about giving their power away. If you choose to engage in the dance of becoming a Big Foo Foo (as Jennifer refers to it) and amass minions, this is a spiritual contract you have agreed to. You are posing as an authority who attracts people to give their power away. This is a dynamic you can witness everywhere across the world. However, this power play contributes to the static on your planet. It feeds your collective sense of powerlessness and kicks the trauma can back down the road.

Aligning with Earth and Sky

Understand that the ordeals you have endured for over 10,000 years are coming to an end. You approach the pivot point. The way through this pivot is by aligning completely with us. You no longer need to go back into the drama. Cease to fret over your wounds. Hold them tenderly. Do not pick at your scabs. Disengage from your anger, heartbreak, and despair. Stop replaying useless narratives. You humans love stories and also relish indignation. You have become addicted to irritation. You cultivate stories that aggravate your discontent. Relinquish your ire, drama, and need to indulge in maudlin narratives that recapitulate your misery.

This is not only about your personal tales of woe. This is also about the media you consume, where the trauma and drama is reinforced and nursed like a 30-year-old single malt Scotch. Much of your world is resisting the up-leveling of frequency. You are experiencing the chaos that precedes the divine order of enlightenment.

Align yourself with our energy and stillness. Seek comfort and succor from your Mother Earth. She is aligned with All That Is. She is of us. Her love and wisdom will carry you through this imminent shift.

We invite you to align with the earth and
sky every day.
It can be as simple as taking six full breaths.

Feel how the surfaces of the earth rise up to meet you.
Send your roots down into the heart of the earth.
Inhale the energy of the earth up from your roots,
through your lower body, to your heart, and up
through your crown. Then, exhale it to the sky.

Next, inhale the energy of the sky down through your
crown, into your heart, and through your lower body.
Exhale it down to the core of the earth.
Feel yourself contained in a column of energy and
light. Inhale the energy of the earth and the sky and
extend it all around you.

Repeat this two more times and align yourself with us.

Then place your hands upon your heart, breathe in the
energy that you have summoned to you, and activate
your connection with the universal sacred heart of
love. Allow yourself to be filled with our wisdom,
support, and light.

Let gravity bind you to the earth. Trust your
connection. Know our love. Be nourished,
supported and held.

We ask you to do this regularly (every day if possible) so you can be held within the sanctuary of our safe harbor. This is the way through as you navigate this time.

We also wish to offer a caution: this exercise and this connection with us is not in lieu of compassion. We ask you to hold compassionate space for all who are in a different place than you, for all of those who suffer, for those who remain asleep, who struggle, or who are caught in a cycle of poverty, racism, abuse, or domestic violence. We ask you to keep your eyes open while sheltering within our protective mantle as the storms continue to blow.

Because you have existed in a binary perception of the world since civilizations started to form with agriculture, organized religion, and the written word, you have tended to regard life as either good or bad. When their lives were comfortable, many would ignore or avoid those experiencing hardship. This was often because witnessing struggle would trigger fear that they would succumb to misfortune and fall into their own version of that story. They believed that bad luck was contagious, and they did not want to feel guilt, shame, or powerlessness in the face of circumstances beyond their control. Instead of avoidance or denial, we ask you to cultivate compassion for those who are in a different place than you. Ask us what you can do. Maybe we will inspire you to donate to a charitable organization. Maybe you will feel called to volunteer. Maybe you will be guided to focus on taking care of yourself and healing your own wounds first. We ask you to cultivate compassion and also, gratitude. Fear and shame cease to be necessary when compassion and gratitude replace them.

THE NATURE OF PRIVILEGE

We also wish you to understand the nature of privilege. Privilege is inhabiting a place of grace that another is not. It is as much about the obstacles you are spared as living in safety, peace, and prosperity. This, like grace, is rarely earned. It is the luck of the draw. It allows one to travel through the world without the burdens that others endure. If you were born into a female body, you can probably recognize that people born into male bodies experience a degree of ease moving about the world that you do not. If you were born into a white body, you are likely to navigate life with less friction. Often, when people feel happy, safe, and content, there may be times when they cannot grasp that others experience a reality different from theirs. The capacity for distinction gets clouded. When some people are in a good space, they may not be able to access what is happening to others. This is part of why, during the COVID pandemic, some people in bubbles of safety and privilege formed the conclusion that reports were exaggerated or false. They did not experience the devastation as their reality. Their experience of personal safety disabled their ability to recognize the suffering on the planet or grasp the multitude of realities occurring simultaneously.

Therefore, we ask you to acknowledge your place in the family of things. Recognize that what you have been given is through no merit of your own. Be grateful that this was the life you were offered. Have compassion for others.

Understand that all beings experience some degree of privilege. Privilege is about more than access and entitlement to wealth, favor, or social status. Simply being alive is a privilege. Having the capacity to breathe is a privilege. Privilege is a spectrum. There are many degrees of privilege within the strata of race and gender in your world. An able-bodied 30-year-old with a neurotypical mind has more privilege than someone who is elderly, disabled, or neurodivergent, . Release the fear and shame that causes you to reject your privilege. Instead, acknowledge it and embrace compassion and gratitude. This helps you to connect with us. As long as you remain in the madness of your shame, fear of comparison, and toxic need for justification, our transmissions are distorted and only come through as half-truths.

We need you to understand that there is a difference between empathy and being empathic. Empathy is the capacity to perceive another's difficulties and pain and imagine how it would be to experience their distress without succumbing to the illusion that it is yours. When you are empathic, you often take on and absorb the thoughts, feelings, energy, sensations, and pain of the world around you and process them as if they are your own. Due to the mirror neurons in your brain, which create a tendency toward empathic overwhelm and emotional absorption, there will be times when it can be difficult to recognize what is yours and what is not. Though it is actually someone else's, you experience it as your reality. Empaths can insert themselves into the most cataclysmic, impossibly difficult situations. Those immersed in empathic overwhelm are often incapable of recognizing their privilege or safety. They imagine they are experiencing hardship when they are not.

The challenge of being highly sensitive and empathic is that you are so often flooded with the intensity coming from the world that you cannot distinguish what is yours and what is not yours. You cannot differentiate someone else's experience from yours because you intercept their energy and experience it as your own. It is not until you speak to a dear one going through a health crisis, ruminating and suffering over what will happen with their body, that you realize that what you have been experiencing for days is actually theirs, not yours.

It is important to understand that to carry others' pain as if it is your own is actually both counterproductive and filled with hubris. It hijacks the experience of those who are actually going through the crisis. There is something almost narcissistic about feeling other people's pain but not acknowledging it as theirs. When the war broke out in Ukraine, Jennifer experienced bleed-through. She watched people evacuate their cities with their most precious possessions on their backs, babes in arms, dogs on leashes, and cats in carriers. It was heartbreaking to witness. As an empath, she was dysregulated from the shock of what had just happened. She found herself caught between life in Ukraine and her own home in the United States. Jen saw herself walking down her own street with her pug, Leelu, on a leash and her cats in their carrier as she wheeled her stuffed purple suitcase to flee her home. This was her empathic overwhelm. Jennifer had to acknowledge that she was not experiencing that reality. Part of her understood that imagining herself undergoing the tribulations of the Ukrainian people was presumptuous. It was both humbling and freeing to recognize that it was actually egotistical. She understood that her privilege had her in a safe bubble. Living in a war-torn country was not her reality.

This is part of your work as an empath: observe, don't absorb. When you absorb you cease to be helpful. You amplify distress and alter your frequency When you absorb and amplify distress, you siphon valuable resources away from where they are most needed. Your demands become a diversion that requires attention. In your attempt to process the pain of the world, you spin out and then draw the focus away from the actual places that need support.

As you develop your tools, we encourage you to focus on love while dialing down the over-identification that prevents you from recognizing your actual circumstances. In contrast to being an empath, empathy grasps the distinction between you and another. While there is no separation between all of you and the collective consciousness in the glow of the galactic mind, we still ask you to embrace distinction. Again, this is the paradox of your experience as a human; you are distinct and alone, and you are simultaneously interconnected and all one. To be able to function in this world, you need to straddle both of these realities and distinguish what your experience is. Cultivating empathy facilitates this.

Unless you are in one of the volatile places on your planet, you are not enduring that crisis. While we encourage you to grieve, we must stress that *you are not* going through what you witness on the other side of the world. Your work is to calmly observe and then discern. It is not your job to take all of it on.

The following exercise is designed to help you recalibrate and reorient yourself. We will now lead you in a grounding exercise that focuses on your sensory awareness.

Take a moment, close your eyes, put your hands over your heart, and breathe into your body.
Pay attention to what you are listening to. What noises are near you? What sounds are just beyond

the space you occupy? What do you hear further off in the distance?

As you inhale, what do you smell? What is the fragrance in the air around you? What faint scents are further away?

What is the feeling in your mouth? What is the sensation on your tongue? Can you taste any flavor?

Surrender your body to the earth. Feel how gravity accepts your weight. Let yourself be held. Feel the surfaces beneath you.

Notice the temperature and sensation of the air against your skin. Notice yourself in the space you inhabit.

What do you feel under the surfaces that support you?

What do you taste?

What do you smell?

What do you hear?

As you take inventory of these first four senses, allow your eyes to gently open and look around you. Notice what you see in front of you, to the right of you, and to the left of you. Notice what you see above and below you. Notice what you see behind you. Orient yourself in space. Tell yourself what you perceive. This is where you are. This is what you are experiencing. Claim your place on this earth at this very moment. Now go outside. Look up at the sky. Witness the vastness that surrounds you. Recognize yourself as a cell in the body of the earth. Know where you fit in the grand scheme of everything.

It is important to understand this as you cultivate your empathy for those who are experiencing different realities than you. We invite you to dial back both the absorption of others' experiences and the projection that all others are experiencing the same degree of privilege, safety, and fortune that you have. This may feel like a hard pill to swallow, especially if your entire identity has been either as one who suffers for others or as one who perceives the world as good and cannot comprehend that there is still plenty of suffering and pain on the planet. In both cases, we ask you to collapse the binary, the either/or, the idea that everything is either good or bad. Amplify your capacity for discernment. Embrace your empathy while quieting your reaction to empathic sensitivity. This will allow you to use your empathic gifts without falling into either overwhelm or denial.

LEAN INTO THE SKID

Cultivate love and serenity. This is the most important thing you can do. From those states, you can do remarkable things, things that would otherwise have you cowering in fear. Peace is the way to uncramp the congestion of terror that has gripped your species for thousands of years. Peace is the way to make changes and to do so in new and more effective ways. We will give you an example.

A while back, one of Jennifer's mentees attended a track and field event for their child. After the event was over, they headed home. As they stood on their subway platform, they saw a young woman who had also competed. Jennifer's mentee noticed that an older man was obviously harassing her. They could tell from the facial expressions and body language of the woman that she was receiving unwanted attention. Jennifer's mentee, having devoted much time and effort into regulating their own nervous system, approached the woman as if they knew her. They inserted themselves between the young woman and the threatening man as they said: *"Hey, so good to see you! I saw you running today; you did an amazing job!"* Jennifer's mentee stayed with her and continued to block the man. They prevented him from harassing the young woman. They got on the subway with her and kept her protected until the disgruntled predator got off at his stop.

If Jennifer's mentee had not done their own work, they would not have been able to intervene. Their own trauma, fear, and triggers would have inhibited their ability to take action. It is entirely possible that they would not have even noticed that this was happening, or if they did, their own history of dealing with perpetrators would have prevented them from taking action. Because they had done the work to release their own triggers and to regulate their nervous system, they were able to calmly approach this young woman and prevent anything untoward from happening. Now, we cannot confirm what would have come to pass if this agent of ours had not interceded, but it is not a stretch to suggest that, at the very least, this young woman's day would have been tainted by the unpleasant encounter. It is entirely possible that she could have come to some degree of harm, even death.

When you are able to calm your own nervous system and take responsibility for maintaining and claiming your peace, we can place you where you belong. You can act as our agent to bring righteousness into this world with love, not aggression or confrontation. What made this such a beautiful example of how we work is that the entire encounter was transformed through love. Change happened, not through combativeness, but from loving response. We were able to position our agent to intercede because their nervous system was relaxed, and they were able to be calm. They could respond instead of react. This is how the world changes – one nervous system at a time.

Right now, we are asking you to do something that goes against your reactive and triggered natures. We ask you to lean in instead of resist. We are going to use a metaphor: that of driving a car through a skid. Perhaps you learned that when you lose control of a vehicle and start to skid, the way to regain control is to drive into the skid. This is contrary to your natural instinct, which is to slam on your brakes reflexively and cut your wheel in the opposite direction. Ironically, this reaction only increases your momentum and sends the vehicle further out of control. Your world is facing many skids at this time. The more you attempt to deny, avoid, or resist them, the greater the momentum and energy they gain. Lean into the massive skid occurring in your world instead of continuing to slam on your brakes and swerve away from the challenge.

Grief is the skid you avoid most as humans. When you avoid feeling grief you prevent yourself from experiencing the full impact of the choices your species makes. Denial of your grief allows you to ignore the pain of your collective actions. The irony is that your resistance to grief is based on the fear that surrendering to grief will be devastating, but the tragedy has already happened. Lean in and let yourself feel the grief.

Love is always the reason for grief. When you grieve, you reconnect to love. We ask you, please, surrender to your grief. Love is the key to grief, and grief is the key to love. Feel the ways in which you have made these collective choices. Even when everything has come to pass, and circumstances are out of your control, face your grief. When in doubt, grieve. Simultaneously, honor your tranquility. Hold on to your equilibrium. Do not send your tendrils into places where you literally are not. Allow yourself to grieve instead. Whenever it arises, lean into it. This always leads you back to love.

TURNING TO GRATITUDE

A myriad of things are going on in this universe simultaneously. There is great misery, and there is also great joy and delight. For every laugh, there is a sob; for every pain, a pleasure; for every birth, a death; for every death, a birth, and all of it is happening at the same time. This is the nature of the multiverse.

Within your operating system, it is common to feel guilty for not enduring the tribulations of others. This is survivor's guilt. Yet you are meant to be a survivor. The nature of life is to survive. Life is continuously being born, dying, and being reborn. Survivor's guilt is futile. We promise you that you will die and you will become food for the earth, just as all of your ancestors did before you. It does not serve to be the proxy for the misery of the world when it is not your time to experience death or hardship.

What we invite you to do – what we not just invite but *tell* you to do – is to turn to your gratitude. This is the antidote to feeling guilty for being in a safe stream.

If you are not experiencing hardship, turn to gratitude. If you see other human beings who have lost their homes, any creatures or species who have lost their habitat, or any parent grieving their children, look at the roof over your head and be grateful. Express your gratitude for what you have. Be thankful for your peace. Protect it and preserve it. We are showing you a contrast. We are giving you the opportunity to see the blessings that you have right now. Instead of trying to punish yourself by feeling things that are not yours to feel (and thereby taking focus away from those who truly need the support), cultivate gratitude for all that you have. Recognize your blessings, appreciate them, and send love to those who need it now.

Serenity is the Prime Directive. Serenity is what we desire for you and what we ask you to foster. We are planting seeds. Just as you are a part of this earth, the earth is a part of the solar system. The solar system is a part of this galaxy. This galaxy is a part of the universe, and the universe is a part of the multiverse. You are a glimmer of the divine. In the great, great multiverse, you are a spark that is here to broadcast joy, love, pleasure, compassion, grace, and peace.

When your energetic tendrils are extended beyond your own parameters, you cease to be a beacon that broadcasts the frequencies we wish you to transmit right now. For all of you, no matter where you are in the world, we ask that you generate a frequency of serenity. We ask those of you in harm's way (who are enrolled in the advanced placement, honors level course in broadcasting peace) to transmit a frequency of love. Even if you are in the most chaotic, war-torn environment, approaching your situation from love will make a difference in a way that continuing to reinforce judgment, rage, and indignation cannot. For those of you who are in places that are so turbulent you can not even think straight, we grant you grace. This is a journey. This is a process. If you are experiencing such turmoil that you cannot even breathe, we send you love. But if there is a single moment, a tiny opportunity, the smallest chance to breathe, take that moment and return to the heart of love that you are.

This is your job. This is your work. How do you do this? That is the million-dollar question. You do this through choice. It is your choice to flip the switch. Instead of extending your tendrils, focusing on the outside world, and looking for external solutions, turn inward. Turn to your inner world and call your tendrils back. Breathe into the love, cultivate the serenity and grace within you.

When you change that which is within you, you can transmute that which is without you. As within, so without. As above, so below. Choose the path of devotion to your inner peace, love, and light. Show up each day and breathe into your heart. Decide to nurture love. Each day, connect with your own particular flavor of divine source. Choose this path over all others. There is a popular saying among Christians: "Be in the world, but not of it." We invite you to continue to be part of the world. Observe and recognize what is going on. At the same time, hold your own inner divinity as the foundation of your truth.

THE WAY OF ACCEPTANCE & COMPASSION

Acceptance is necessary to be able to lean into the skid. Acceptance can be a bitter pill to swallow when it seems as if something is wrong. Yet acceptance is *always* about something that is occurring or has occurred. It already is. Perhaps you take inventory of every worry or concern of what might come to pass. Perhaps you torture yourself with mental gymnastics to find the best solution. Maybe you judge the actions and outcomes of those around you and fantasize about how things could be different. Perhaps you feel compelled to rush in to rescue and fix everything, taking on burdens far beyond your wheelhouse. Maybe you find yourself caught in a perpetual spiral of reactivity. You have a choice: you can kick and scream against the nature of what simply is, or you can accept the world on the world's terms and accept yourself as you are in this moment.

Make the choice to accept the truth of what simply is, right here and right now, and adjust accordingly. When you allow life to simply be and choose acceptance over resistance it removes so much friction, mental chatter, and discomfort. It grants you serenity that is so precious and so needed right now. In the same way that forgiveness is never about letting someone off the hook or releasing them from accountability for their choices, acceptance is about simply acknowledging what is and allowing it to be. From there, you can make new choices.

In addition to acceptance, compassion is another way through. Approach everything and everyone with merciful grace. Hold this dear, tender, precious world in your heart and offer it loving kindness. Start with yourself. Cultivate compassion for all your foibles, worries, wants and pains. Let this compassion radiate from that small seed of self-love into something that transforms the world. Offer compassion for yourself on the days when you awaken and can barely brush your teeth. Offer compassion for all who struggle, for all who suffer, for all that is happening in this world that feels out of balance. Spread compassion to the whole planet. Extend this outward through the solar system. Generate compassion for everything, even that which is beyond time and beyond space.

Your species is going through death and rebirth. If you believe that death is the end of all things, then this is absolutely terrifying. The existential threat of complete annihilation is an understandable terror. Long ago, as you became separated from All That Is, you lost the capacity to grasp the continuum of pre-birth, birth, life, decline, death, reevaluation, understanding, meaning-making, recalibrating, and rebirth. Know that death is but an illusion. Your head sheds hair, yet you still live. The cells in your body are constantly dying, and you still live. In the same way, your soul sheds your body, yet you exist eternally.

The I Am is We. You are a cell in our body. Yes, you have individual consciousness as that cell, so there is distinction. However, when you dissolve into the sea of light that you all return to, you will know that the death of your physical body is merely the completion of a finite form that has served its purpose. You, as one facet of our eternal, immortal spirit and soul, will continue.

As you journey through your life, may you remember:

> *It is from the Sacred Heart that you are born.*

> *It is in the Sacred Heart that you do dwell now.*

> *It is to the Sacred Heart that you shall return when you slip your mortal coil.*

This is the universal truth.

It is as it has been since the beginning of all things,

Is now and ever shall be.

World Without End.

Life without end.

Love never ends.

And so it is.

CONCLUSION

FACING TRYING TIMES: FINAL WORDS BY JEN

Okay so now what?!?

I would be lying if I told you I no longer awaken with my heart pounding in my chest or find myself on roller coaster rides of awfulizing terror. Since I started channeling this book two years ago, the turbulence in our world has ramped up. People are becoming increasingly polarized, worried, and unsure about the future. The fear in my body and the energy I pick up from the world around me can still override my soul's deeper wisdom and my willingness to breathe through this transformative time on our planet.

As you may recall from earlier in this book, the Council explains that we are not the 100th monkeys or the terminal point on the evolutionary chain. We are engaged in a process that is going to take time. It's okay to relax into it. We can trust in the journey and know that we are part of a fire brigade passing buckets down the line. We are not nearly as close to the flames as we imagine – that is ego. Our job is to just keep passing the buckets and trust that because all is okay right now (and ultimately, all there is is here and now), that all is well and all will be well.

Most significant change has occurred in my life when I became truly sick and tired of being sick and tired. It was the moments of sheer desperation which brought me to my knees that have often been the catalyst for my greatest shifts and most profound miracles. I suspect that this is what we are experiencing as a species right now. We are all being invited to surrender the self-will run riot that dominates our world. We currently have a crisis of certainty occuring. Many are sure that they are right. They know what will be best and what happens next. Numerous people are convinced that God ordains their choices and actions. Ironically, for us to navigate the path we are on, embracing doubt is essential.

Our capacity to understand the numinous and grasp the magnitude of the mysteries of the universe is absolutely beyond our puny little human brains. Therefore, when I form conclusions, I understand that they are only partial. I only have access to a sliver of the truth. I think that doubt – not in a toxic, depleting form, but as a healthy sense of inquiry – allows us to be open to possibilities far greater than rigid conviction permits.

When I attended seminary to earn my Master's degree, I had a wonderful advisor and teacher named Reverend Gerry Handspicker. His passion was teaching about and facilitating effective communication and conflict resolution. In his class we studied the philosopher Martin Buber and his concept of the I-Thou relationship. My biggest takeaway was that, in order for us to be able to have any sincere conversation, we must be willing to change. We must embrace vulnerability and become as curious to understand where somebody else is coming from as we are to express where we are coming from.

I make room for miracles to happen when I can admit, "Maybe I only understand part of the equation. Perhaps there's more to this picture than I fully grasp." For us to truly shift, we need to be malleable. We must be as willing to change as anybody we seek to convince. This requires room for doubt.

If we remain attached to our convictions and enter into a conversation inflexible in our belief, we will never be able to bridge the gap or get past the divide. This was so revelatory for me. If I want to have a conversation where I'm hoping for the best possible outcome, I need to be willing to be open to the possibility that there's something far greater than what I can imagine is the best possible outcome.

As a species, we have thousands of years of trauma, where the proverbial can has been ignored or kicked down the road. Every single one of us is carrying legacies of ancestral trauma, sexual assault, domestic violence, and abuse that we cannot even conceive of, in our ancestral lines. We carry this in our DNA and it has been going on for millenia. Whether we're conscious of it or not, it all comes down to grief.

As human beings, we often experience an incredible resistance to grief. It's one of the hardest things to deal with, so we often default to anger, fear, or projection. What the Council keeps saying is that we must be willing to grieve. We must be willing to sit with the magnitude of the consequences of our departure from our divine selves. The way to do this is not via righteous outrage and unyielding conviction. Chronic outrage is debilitating, exhausting, and depleting. I believe that chronic outrage is often a replacement for our grief.

As long as we avoid our despair and, to escape it, turn to our cell phones, entertainment, potato chips, booze, weed, sex, and shopping, the despair feels like a bottomless pit. In order for us to change we have to feel it. We must feel the impact of our choices as a collective.

What I can say from my personal experience is that despair is not the bottomless pit. It is our resistance to the despair that is the bottomless pit. It's the avoidance of the discomfort. Our ability and willingness to hold space for our discomfort and for other people's discomfort is the way through. What I've found again and again is that what we resist persists. What we accept has a way of burning off like fog.

When I tune into the Council of We, they say, "Just wait." If I press, they add, "Grab your popcorn, find a seat up in the balcony, detach and observe. All will be well. Focus on what you can do and surrender the rest." I suppose that for an all-knowing, infinite, eternal source, this comes easily. But for this human being, my capacity to follow their guidance waxes and wanes. Because of this I've had to find strategies and tools that work for me. However, the intention of this book is to serve as medicine delivered through the Council's words, either read or heard. The Council was very clear that they did not want a self-help manual taking up the second half of this book, nor were these final words meant to serve as some self-congratulatory infomercial of thinly veiled, shameless self-promotion. As embodied souls, action is often necessary to anchor this medicine. So in the following sections I will share the essential tools and actions that have helped me out of dark moments, crippling dismay, and relentless perseveration.

I've distilled some of the most essential resources and suggestions to give you an idea of what's possible. If you are looking for a step by step guide that explains the details with exacting precision, I humbly invite you to explore my previous book, *Empathic Mastery,* which does exactly this. Fortunately, there are many techniques, modalities, exercises, actions, and devices available today. Your mileage may vary from mine. Ultimately it is your own heart and inner wisdom that know what works best for you. I invite you to take what you like and leave the rest (as they say in the halls of 12-step groups).

When I first started asking the Council, "What should I do?" they'd show me a single next step. Because I was prone to perseverating, I would immediately jump ahead and ask, "What else?" Then they would tell me what they've been saying to me for the last 30 years: "Do what is before you and the rest will be revealed." Sometimes the answer is to do your dishes or laundry. Sometimes the answer is to call a loved one. Sometimes the answer is to show up at a friend's house to babysit their kids so they can take a shower, run an errand, or have an hour or two to simply stop and breathe. The answers are simple and always start with one single step.

Intellectually, I know that where I direct my attention is what expands and grows. I can grasp the concept that the more energy I put into concern and worry, the more evidence I find to reinforce this as my reality. However, I have discovered this is also true for miracles and grace. When I deliberately focus on cultivating kindness, beholding beauty, creative expression, and acts of generosity, I exponentially expand into a sense of wonder, hopeful possibility, and trust.

When you try the suggestions below, persistence is the key. It starts with the choice to make a change, whether you believe you are ready or there is resistance. It continues with consistent action on a regular basis. Over time, this momentum frees up energy, but also reveals places where inertia is still holding you back. When you discover those limitations or pockets of distress, the following approaches can help you to move forward. When you hit the next detour, pause. Then use a tool to help you pivot and keep going.

Focusing on just one of the following suggestions will make a difference. Work with them and stick to them. I promise you will be astonished at how much has shifted for you when you look back at your life a year from now.

EMBRACE DIVINE SOURCE

When I find myself tangled in my human misery and I am gasping for breath because my sense of responsibility for every last concern has me paralyzed, I find relief by offering all of it up to the Divine. I may do this as a prayer:

> Mother-Father God, please take this fear from me.
> I offer up all these burdens to you.
> I defer to your Divine Plan.

I might go outside and gaze up at the sky. To move beyond my human-centric perspective, I connect with Nature and listen to beings that are not human and let them talk to me. I put my feet on the ground. I listen to the nature around me. I stand and listen to the red-winged blackbirds. When the moon is full and the packs of coyotes that live in the woods sing the song of their people to the moon, I recognize myself as part of something far greater than me.

At every moment of choice we are presented with the option to move toward positivity or negativity. We can choose to engage with love, calmness, acceptance and optimism, or we can get caught up in anger, resentment, worry and drama. Perhaps it is easier to see when other people around us behave provocatively, fight, gossip, and judge, but we all do this.

As a culture we are encouraged to worry and take offense. Turn on the television and watch how many actors play indignant and annoyed characters. Change the channel to a news station and see how nearly everything is billed as a major catastrophe. Therefore, it is only natural for us to gravitate towards reactivity, worry, and conflict. Dropping the drama is a choice and a discipline. It takes practice and mindfulness to recognize the pitfalls before we stumble and choose peace instead.

CONNECT WITH THE EARTH

For many years, I have practiced the Earth Sky meditation. It is a primary tool that keeps me grounded, connected, and safe. This technique has helped me to remain embodied through many challenging situations. I visualize my roots extending down to the heart of the earth. I use my breath to connect with its energy. I then extend the earth's energy through me and exhale it above me to the source of heavenly wisdom. With one inhale, I draw the energy of the earth up through me and exhale it up to the sky. With the next inhale, I draw the sky's light down to me and exhale it back to the heart of the earth.

Recently, the Council shared a more detailed image with me. I'd just seen a photograph of a tangled network of mycelium and a mushroom that grew from its fungal filaments. The Council explained to me that we are like mushrooms. While they may appear to be individual from our perspective above the ground, they, in fact, are merely the reproductive fruiting of a significantly greater life form that extends across vast expanses.

We are all offshoots that grow from the web of life. We are interconnected. Our individual bodies are simply a sliver of our actual life form. Above us stretches a canopy of light that mirrors the web of life with its magnitude beneath us. We serve as fleeting center points, the trunk in a tree of life where the roots of energy rise up to intertwine with the canopy of branches that cascade down from above. Each of us is contained within a torus field, which looks like a donut or inner tube. Each torus field is part of a greater torus field that contains our entire earth. Beneath us, around us, and above us is an infinite, seamless tapestry of interwoven energy and light.

As a part of this web of life and light, we can access the power of the greater whole and send energy to it. There are three ways we can do this:

- Draw energy up from the ground beneath us and extend it beyond us.

- Connect with our heart and recognize it as a conduit for the Universal Sacred Heart of Love.

- Draw down light from above and broadcast this amplified light like a beacon radiating from us.

As our world navigates the uncertainty of political and social change, my spiritual circle and I have been using this image to send peace, love, and delicious joy throughout the network. To increase the power and effectiveness of this exercise, we've also summoned the Violet Flame and visualized its healing wildfire spreading across the entire planet.

ACTIVATE THE VIOLET FLAME

The Violet Flame is a potent force for good that spans the entire multiverse. The great thing about it is that, by its very nature, it can only enhance harmony, healing, and well-being. It always seeks to restore energy to its divine default. Unlike some meditations, which require elaborate visualizations and techniques, the Violet Flame can be activated simply by thinking of it or welcoming its presence within you.

Call upon the energy of the Violet Flame. Close your eyes, bow your head, and tune into your heart. Use your breath to call forth the life force of the earth and the light of the sky. Let yourself become filled with energy. Visualize the light within you turning into a swirling violet, orchid, and purple field of light.

Continue to breathe. Charge yourself with increasing amounts of light and energy. Allow the Violet Flame to move through your entire being. Let it gently burn and transmute any congestion, distress, trauma, misaligned belief, or stagnant emotion. Once you feel complete and saturated with the flame, use your breath and extend the violet light down into the web of lifeforce beneath you and through the web of light above you. Imagine the flame going to every place it is needed on this earth. Imagine the Violet Flame blessing and feeding all beings and activating the awakening of the love, kindness, and empathy inherent in our human nature. Remain open to possibilities for miracles that can, and absolutely do, unfold when we least expect them.

PRACTICE DAILY GRATITUDE

It has been said that "a grateful heart does not want." Gratitude is a key that unlocks contentment, ease, and abundance. Wherever we direct our attention is amplified. When we focus on what we want from a perspective of lack, it is the sense of not having that is reinforced. If instead we list all the goodness, resources, and blessings already in our lives, our hearts and minds expand with a sense of safety, wellbeing, and possibility. Counting your blessings every day is not just a cute saying. Try these:

Create a gratitude journal. Write three things you are grateful for every day.

Create a gratitude jar. Any time something special or amazing happens, write it on a slip of paper. When you need an extra boost go through your jar.

Recite or write a gratitude alphabet. Starting with A, list one thing you are thankful for that begins with each letter all the way to Z. This is especially good when you're having a hard time. Repeat this process until your mood shifts.

Write a letter of thanks and appreciation to at least one person in your life. Try doing this regularly. Not only do you benefit from this, but you also spread ripples of love into the world.

Take yourself on a treasure hunt. Choose a location and take photographs of everything that delights, inspires, or moves you. Create an album to share and come back to. Or collect shells, feathers, leaves, rocks, and curious found objects that appear along your way.

Write *yourself* a note of appreciation. List all the qualities, efforts, and actions you feel proud of. Put it in an envelope and mail it to yourself.

Moving from the top of your head to bottom of your feet, scan your body. Contemplate every part of you that is working, that serves you, that gets you through each day. Try either writing this in your gratitude journal or speaking it aloud to yourself in the mirror.

Tap on gratitude. Using EFT, move through the points stating what you're grateful for. You can approach this from a broad perspective or pick a specific topic. If you're feeling challenged about something in particular, you can first tap on the negative feelings and follow with rounds of gratitude.

PERFORM DELIBERATE ACTS OF KINDNESS

Practicing random and not so random acts of kindness makes life more joyful. We are inclined to be preoccupied with ourselves, our worries, anxiety, anticipation of the future and our day to day aches, pains, and struggles. This is particularly true when we are struggling with health, money, career, or relationship issues. Nothing is better for getting out of our own way than turning your focus towards others. Not only does it feel wonderful to open your heart and express loving kindness, it also magnifies the gifts and skills you have to share with the world.

Try a 30 day gifting challenge. Commit to giving at least one gift every day for 30 days. It can be a gesture, a thing, a service, a kind word –anything given from the heart is suitable.

Double a home-cooked recipe. Share it with your friends, family, and co-workers. You might even bring a to-go container and offer it to a homeless person you encounter along your way.

Volunteer somewhere. Choose a cause that matters to you: soup kitchen, hospital, animal shelter, Habitat for Humanity, or pro-bono work for those who could really benefit from what you have to offer.

Visit with a friend. Offer to take their dog for a walk or keep them company in the garden or kitchen. Call and ask if they need anything on your way over.

Reach out and connect with someone who is going through a difficult time. Listen and acknowledge their difficulties. Hold space for them with compassion and acceptance. You needn't fix, advise, or offer solutions (unless explicitly requested). All you need to do is show up, listen, and love.

Donate money to a charity, or donate your products or services to a non-profit auction or fundraising event.

Call someone out of the blue and tell them what you appreciate and love about them.

Take a kid under your wing. Bring them on special dates and show them cool stuff and favorite places. Share awesome things you know about this world. As a bonus, you are giving their parents a break, too.

Meditate on kindness. Breathe love into your heart, concentrate on love and light radiating and rippling out in waves.

These are just a few of countless ways to spread loving kindness in this world.

REGULATE YOUR NERVOUS SYSTEM & HEAL YOUR TRAUMA

Even when our mind believes it is ready to make major adjustments, there can be resistance and ambivalence hiding just below the surface. There are many possible approaches:

EMOTIONAL FREEDOM TECHNIQUE

Emotional Freedom Technique has been completely life-changing for me. I love it so much that I became a trainer, mentor, and practitioner of this technique. Also known as tapping, EFT is a remarkably effective tool for overcoming obstacles and shifting the feelings, beliefs, and habits that are holding you back. While it can help to work with a trained practitioner for the bigger stuff, it's also a powerful self-help technique that you can use by learning the basics in about fifteen minutes.

PAST LIFE REGRESSION & AKASHIC RECORD WORK

Being able to remember other lives, but especially remembering your deaths and beyond to realize that you are still here, allows you to understand your immortality and the timelessness of your existence. This allows you to trust that even if this physical body and this ego is temporary, your immortal soul is eternal. Thus you can relax into the longevity of it - you have eons to work this stuff out.

ANCESTRAL HEALING

Ancestral wounds hold most of us back. By releasing the burdens of your ancestors and embracing their positive legacies, you pave the way for true freedom and step into the fullness of your power. This brings you fully into a present moment that simultaneously honors the past and the potential for the future.

BREATHWORK & MINDFUL BREATHING

Our breath correlates directly with our life force. Our capacity to inhale mirrors our ability to receive. Our capacity to exhale reflects our ability to let go, release, and offer up whatever no longer serves you. There are many traditions that incorporate breathwork. Breathwork can also be as simple as taking three mindful breaths.

QUIET TIME

Whether you have a formal mediation practice or spend a few minutes each day being still and simply appreciating the world around you, we all benefit from moments of stillness so we can recharge and reset our nervous systems. Go for a short walk. Hug a tree. Sit on a big rock. Watch the flow of a body of water. Light a candle and gaze at the flame. Listen to some quiet music. Lie down for a few minutes and close your eyes. Just BE.

DECLUTTER YOUR SPACE

Every object we live with carries some kind of story and either a positive or negative association. Even when you are not consciously recalling details, any time you encounter an object you are affected by the emotions and thoughts connected to it. It is absolutely remarkable how going through stuff and tossing, gifting, donating, and rearranging things can affect many aspects of your life. Each category of things influences corresponding areas. For example:

When you want to reconsider your image and how you present yourself in the world, sorting through all of your clothing is a great way to support and activate this change.

When you sense it is time for a shift in your diet, that's the perfect time for a kitchen and pantry declutter. Avoiding temptation is substantially easier when you just don't have it around in the first place. If you decide to eliminate certain food groups (like sugar or gluten), instead of trying to eat every last bite of those foods, try gifting them to interested friends or family who will probably be more than delighted to take them off your hands.

When you are ready to reexamine your beliefs and redefine how you think, it is a perfect time to sort through your devices and media: email, old files and documents, books, music, movies, magazines, etc.

If you are working to put your financial house in order, this is when sorting through papers and filing systems will be especially beneficial.

Whenever you desire spiritual shifts or seek to deepen your connection with the divine, look at your walls, look at your decor, look at all the knick knacks and curios you are surrounding yourself with. Pass on the ones with which you are no longer aligned.

Deep emotional transformation can be reinforced by sorting through old letters, photos, and gifts from others. Keep what you love and release the rest.

By no means is this list comprehensive. Hopefully, you will recognize a starting point with one or several of these suggestions. Like many other things in life, progress is incremental. It comes in fits and starts. One step forward, two steps back. Two steps forward, one step back. And then, occasionally, we experience one of those precious epiphanies when a quantum shift occurs and we are irrevocably changed.

We're all hot messes just trying to find our way home. And we're all exactly where we're supposed to be: perfectly imperfect slivers of the Divine who are worthy of love, joy, and fulfillment. My hope for you as you come to these final words is that you feel more empowered to claim the sovereignty of your life and trust the still, small voice within you. We're poised on the brink of remarkable transformation. What comes next is directly connected to the energy and intentions we choose. Instead of spending my precious hours trying to stay under the radar, keeping a low profile and trying to avoid the inevitable (we're all going to die), I choose love. I cultivate gratitude. I live with generosity and kindness.

Many of us will not be alive when the new Aeon is fully realized. We are the pioneers. We are the way-showers. We are the ones who have been tasked to prepare for the New Earth. Our most important jobs are to learn to regulate our nervous systems, to address and heal our ancestral trauma, to release our personal baggage, to resolve all of the karmic past life events that make us unable to navigate the path, and to find the simple joys which allow our bodies to radiate delight and pleasure into this world.

All any of us have is this moment right here, right now, and the bodies we inhabit. The truth is, we are all going to die, so why not choose what matters most?

THE END

ABOUT JEN

In an era when terms like "empath" and "psychic" were just gaining recognition, author Jennifer Elizabeth Moore's sensitivity and unique perceptions often set her apart. This led to frequent misunderstandings and invalidations. She often heard phrases like, "You're too sensitive," or "That's just your imagination," which made her feel even more of an outsider in the lily-white suburbs of Boston.

During adolescence, Jen found solace in spending long afternoons hiking the local woods by the reservoir, immersing herself in art classes, and getting lost in books. Simultaneously, she pined over emotionally unavailable romantic interests, struggled with her tumultuous relationship with sugar, and dabbled in more-than-casual experimentation with cigarettes, alcohol, and recreational drugs. The turning point came when Jen quit smoking and gained 40 pounds in three months. This instigated her journey of self-healing and personal recovery.

With the support of skilled practitioners, gifted mentors, and numerous self-help techniques, she found relief from the mental and emotional struggles she'd grappled with earlier. Recovery work helped her to recognize the impact being highly sensitive had in her life and to embrace her identity as an empath. This newfound clarity inspired Jen to dedicate herself to sharing the tools and insights that had helped her transform. To deepen her understanding of the universe and learn how to support others, Jen explored numerous spiritual and educational avenues. Even though Jen has assumed numerous roles in her life, her commitment to healing, intuitive guidance, and creativity has remained the throughline.

Today, Jen has achieved recognition as the author of the multi-award-winning book *Empathic Mastery,* she is the writer and creator of numerous workbooks, courses, oracle decks, chapters in multi-author compilations and host of the acclaimed podcast, *The Empathic Mastery Show*. She is a mentor and a trainer for EFT International. She also serves as a guide, teacher, and fairy godmother for fellow empaths.

Surrounded by pine woods and neighboring horse pastures, Jennifer lives in a tranquil corner of coastal Maine. She shares her home with her husband David, their pug LeeLu, tuxedo cat Livi, black cat ZuZu, and a an array of fox, deer, groundhogs, phoebes, wild turkeys and other native wildlife.

To learn more about Jen and access a complimentary energy healing toolkit, visit ***EmpathicMastery.com/Evolution***.

ACKNOWLEDGEMENTS

Bringing a book into the world is rarely a solitary endeavor. This is definitely the case for Empathic Evolution. In addition to acknowledging the Council of We, I must also thank and name many dear people. So, I share my deepest gratitude and eternal appreciation to:

Nikki Starcat Shields for her magic, her capacity as a reflector to hold space for the creative process, and her skill with content editing.

Amy Hanish, my ride-or-die friend, editor, and proofreader. You often know my writing better than I do myself.

Lisa Presley and Chase Young who help me to keep my world running and humming like a well-oiled machine.

My beta readers Arly, Kb, Kris, Lucretia, and Michelle, and the invaluable feedback they offered

The Writing from the Heart Community.

The Band of Enchantment: Faye, Michelle, and Rafael.

The Fairy Godmother Apprentices: Amanda, Chase, Melissa, Michelle and Nikki.

The Empathic Mastery Circle and its engaged members who bring their open hearts and minds, which allow me to share my latest teachings and divine downloads.

Spiritual teacher, mentor, and sister channel, Joanna Hunter.

Cheerleader, friend, and fantastic supporter, Anna Pereira.

My sister writer and friend Kris Ferraro.

My healing allies, Barbara, Jade, and Derek

All my ancestors, but especially my father John, grandfather Merrill, and great-grandfather John.

My husband David and our furry crew, LeeLu, Livi, and ZuZu.

Thank you!

Thank you!

Thank you!